W9-ATJ-742

THE COMPLETE GUIDE TO
WOOD
FINISHES

THE COMPLETE GUIDE TO

WOOD FINISHES

How to apply and restore lacquers, polishes, stains, and varnishes

2nd edition

Technical Consultant: **Mick Allen**
Photographs: **Paul Forrester**

A Fireside Book
Published by Simon & Schuster
New York London Toronto Sydney

Fireside
Rockefeller Center
1230 Avenue of the Americas
New York, NY 10020

Copyright © 2006 by Quarto Publishing Inc.

All rights reserved, including the right of
reproduction in whole or in part in any form.

FIRESIDE and colophon are registered trademarks
of Simon & Schuster, Inc.

For information regarding special discounts for bulk
purchases, please contact Simon & Schuster Special
Sales at 1-800-456-6798 or
business@simonandschuster.com.

Library of Congress Cataloging-in-Publication Data
Allen, Mick.
  The Complete guide to wood finishes : how to
apply and restore lacquers, polishes, stains, and
varnishes / technical consultant: Mick Allen ;
photographs: Paul Forrester.—2nd ed.
    p. cm.
  "A Fireside book."
  Previous ed. by Derrick Crump.
  1. Wood finishing. I. Title: Wood finishes. II.
Crump, Derrick. Complete guide to wood finishes.
III. Title.
TT325.A 42 2006
684.1'043—dc22   2005056328
ISBN-13: 978-0-7432-8487-5
ISBN-10:   0-7432-8487-9

Conceived, designed, and produced by
Quarto Publishing plc
The Old Brewery
6 Blundell Street
London N7 9BH

Project Editors **Paula McMahon and
  Donna Gregory**
Art Editor and Designer **James Lawrence**
Assistant Art Director **Penny Cobb**
Copy Editor **Claire Waite Brown**
Photographer **Paul Forrester**
Illustrator **Kuo Kang Chen**
Proofreader **Claire Waite Brown**
Indexer **Dorothy Frame**

Art Director **Moira Clinch**
Publisher **Paul Carslake**

Manufactured by **Provision Pte Ltd, Singapore**
Printed by **Star Standard Industries Pte Ltd,
  Singapore**

10 9 8 7 6 5 4 3 2 1

Contents

Preparation

Basic finishes

Decorative finishes

Spray finishes

INTRODUCTION

Throughout history, wood has rightly been appreciated as a most useful and versatile natural resource, used across the world for all purposes, from great ships, houses, floors, and furniture to tools, bowls, beads, and toys. In order to get the best qualities from the wood, all wooden items must be finished in some way to preserve and protect the lumber, as well as to bring out the inherent beauty of the grain. However well made an article is, it is by the final finish that it will be judged.

For thousands of years the only treatment was to apply beeswax or oils, or to color the wood with a mixture of pigments and binders to hold the pigment on the surface. Today, an extremely large range of wood finishing products is available, many for specific uses, such as on floors, and others that can be used for a variety of purposes.

SUPERIOR RESULTS ASSURED

While such a wide range of commercial options can only be positive for the wood finisher, it is important to know when and how to apply the basic range of traditional and decorative finishes. This book will take you through the various types of finishes and explains what each should be used for, using illustrated step-by-step sequences to guide you through each process. There has always been a certain mystique about wood finishing but, with a little time and the correct instruction, the amateur can obtain results that in most cases are far superior to the finishes seen on mass-produced furniture. The great thing about wood finishing is that practice really does make perfect!

COMPLETELY UPDATED AND IMPROVED

This book is intended to help everyone who is interested in the craft of wood finishing. It will be useful not only to professional wood finishers, but also to cabinet makers, painters and decorators, DIY enthusiasts, students of the subject, and any other professionals who are interested in protecting the surface of wood. You will learn the basics of surface preparation, tool use and care, how to apply surface coatings and color, and how to restore, repair, or replace damaged finishes.

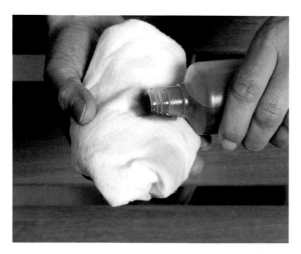

Above: Use oil in the traditional way

Above: Changing the type of finish you use (gloss, semi-gloss, and matte shown here) can have a dramatic effect on the wood

Use the step-by-step instructions to guide you through new processes, or simply to refresh your memory on rusty techniques! With your acquired skills and knowledge you will find wood finishing both worthwhile and extremely satisfying.

Since the first edition of this book was produced, there has been a veritable revolution in the way that we think about the environmental costs of using wood and wood finishes. There is a much greater emphasis nowadays on the utilization of water-based varnishes, and on safe environmental practices. Always consider the environmentally friendly option if one exists, minimize waste, and make sure you dispose of any waste in the appropriate manner— read the instructions that come with the product, or get in touch with your local environmental agency.

Wood finishes that leave a surface film are of three main types. They can dry by evaporation of the solvents, as with French polish; by oxidization and polymerization by absorbing oxygen from the air, as with linseed and other drying oils; or by cross-polymerization, that is, the linking together of the molecules after the addition of the catalyst, as occurs with acid-catalyzed lacquers and two-part polyurethanes. The latter type of product will give the most durable surface, with resistance to heat, solvents, and abrasions. When you are considering what type of finish to apply, always bear in mind to what use the piece you are finishing will be put. For instance, it is not worth using an expensive two-part lacquer on timber wall cladding that will not be subjected to the same wear and tear as would a floor or table top. The golden rule is always to read the manufacturer's instructions, and if using a finish of which you have had no previous experience to experiment on a spare piece of wood.

It is often possible to find old furniture from garage or attic sales, or from auctions, and as long as the basic construction is sound, the finish can be restored to its original or better condition, usually without having to strip back to the bare wood. To see a piece transformed into a thing of beauty, and to know that your work is responsible, is immensely fulfilling. Whether you are working on new furniture or restoring old furniture, you will have a great sense of satisfaction when you see the results you can achieve.

KITTING OUT THE WORKSHOP

The layout, lighting, and heating of the workshop play a vital role in achieving a quality finish. Your workshop must be dry and warm, and have plenty of natural light. There are also a number of jigs, fittings, and ideas for benches and storage that make finishing that much easier.

VENTILATION

Clean air is a must. Your woodshop must be ventilated with opening windows and/or an air filter system. Planning regulations recommend that the area of opening windows must equal 20 percent of the total floor area. If you need to remove fumes and stale air, then you will require a positive pressure ventilation system (PPV).

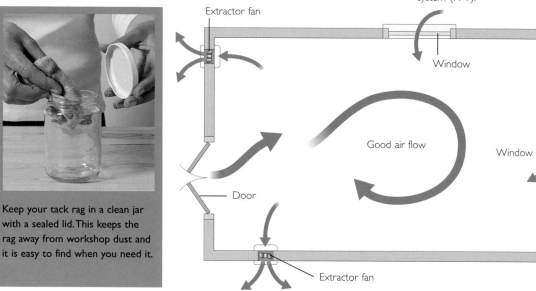

HINTS AND TIPS

Keep your tack rag in a clean jar with a sealed lid. This keeps the rag away from workshop dust and it is easy to find when you need it.

Extractor fan

Window

Good air flow

Window

Door

Extractor fan

In all probability, your finishing workshop is also used for operations such as sawing and sanding, in which case, you will have to ensure that dust is kept under control. A good extractor or industrial vacuum cleaner helps, but make sure the workshop is free from drafts and that nooks and crannies, which serve as dust traps, are kept to a minimum.

STORAGE

The wood finisher's workshop needs ample storage space for holding tools, materials, brushes, rags, and abrasives. Flammable finishes and materials must be kept in a lockable cupboard on their own, out of the way.

Collect airtight containers for storing polishing pads for future use. Do not use old food containers (in case the contents are mistaken for food), or milk bottles. Containers should be labeled carefully and dated. Always have a sealable container at hand for waste materials, which must be disposed of safely (see page 13).

HEATING AND VENTILATION

Manufacturers of most finishing materials advise that the minimum temperature at which their products will dry is about 60°F (16°C). If drying does not take place at the proper rate, defects such as chilling and blushing appear in the surface.

Make sure materials are stored in the workshop for at least one hour before work commences. If it is very cold and you are not able to heat the workshop, use a powerful electric light or a hairdryer to bring the surface temperature nearer to the optimum (the timber will hold the heat for a surprisingly long time).

Finishing materials are designed to flow and are sensitive to heat. If they do not flow, brushmarks are likely to create an uneven coat. Make sure there are no cold drafts, but keep the workshop ventilated to cut down condensation.

WORKBENCH

The workbench can simply be a board on trestles. This helps bring small items and panels up to a convenient height, but can be dismantled when there are large or freestanding pieces in the workshop. Cut up some thin strips of timber on which flat panels can rest while being finished.

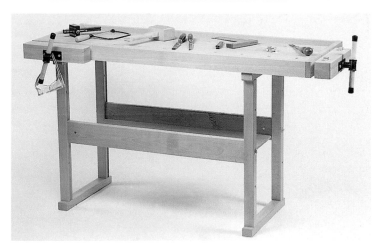

SAFE WORKSHOP SETUP

34 inches

Traditional bench for a man: 34 inches

26-30 inches

Traditional bench for a woman or youth: 26–30 inches

32-33 1/2 inches

Stand-up counter: 32–33 1/2 inches

15-18 inches

Sit-on donkey or shaving horse: 15–18 inches

LIGHTING

When finishing, you will be continually judging color and degree of gloss. To be able to do this successfully, it is essential to have a good light source. The best source is, of course, natural light, which defines subtle differences of color and shade most clearly. This is particularly important when color matching.

If possible, arrange the workshop with northern light, which is constant and natural. Direct sunlight is not advisable, as judging color can be tricky in fierce sunlight. Otherwise, the best alternative to the real thing is to fit fluorescent tubes or light bulbs that give a "natural light."

DRYING RACKS

An important feature of any finishing shop is a drying rack. This can either be fixed or portable, but make sure there is plenty of room for air to circulate between the pieces while they are drying. Doweling jointed into uprights works well for racking, with at least 4 in. (10 cm) between each level. The configuration depends on the type of work you expect to be finishing. For example, chairs need a different set-up to panels—but the principle always remains the same.

MAKING A PAPER BOAT

Boats are traditionally used for mixing and holding small quantities of finish. They are a useful way of using up old sandpaper, and can be disposed of after use.

01 Take a piece of sandpaper 3 x 5 in. (7.5 x 12.5 cm).

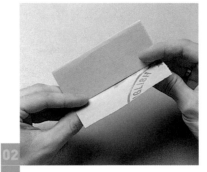

02 Fold in the two long ends.

03 Fold in the two short ends.

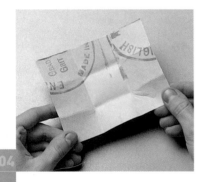

04 Open it out to show the folds.

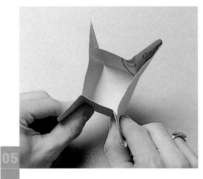

05 Now fold the corners together.

06 Fold the long ends over to hold in shape.

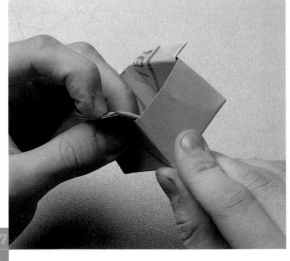

07 Fold over the ends to form a rim.

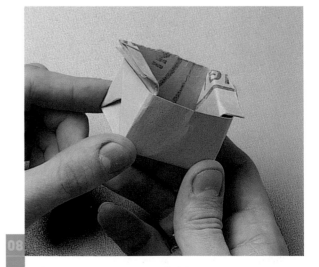

08 Both ends are folded over to hold the container square.

BRUSH CARE

The professional way to clean brushes is to suspend them in a cleaning solution so that the paint literally drops off the end of the bristles without causing damage and bending the bristles out of line. This method will ensure that your expensive brushes last a lot longer, and when you come to use them again, they are like new.

Place the brush on a spare block of wood on a level surface. Drill a small hole through the handle of the brush just above the metal ferrule.

Thread a piece of sturdy wire, or a nail, long enough to stretch the diameter of the neck of the jar, through the hole you've just drilled in the brush.

Submerse the bristles in the cleaning solution, taking care that the solution does not rise above the metal ferrule, otherwise you will saturate the wooden handle. Jiggle the brush gently by the handle to loosen the ingrained paint or varnish and then balance the brush on the wire or nail to keep it upright.

Making sure the bristles do not touch the base of the jar, leave the solution and brush in a well-ventilated space, where it won't get knocked over. If there is room in the jar you can add more brushes to the wire or nail.

The varnish or paint will eventually fall away from the bristles and form a layer at the bottom of the jar. Remove the brushes and wash gently with a mild detergent. To add softness and flexibility to the bristles, you could add ordinary hair conditioner.

When each brush is thoroughly washed and all the residue of varnish or paint has been removed, shake the remaining water from the brush by flicking it a few times. Lay the brush on a piece of kitchen towel.

Wrap the kitchen towel over the end of the brush, keeping the bristles flat and parallel.

With larger brushes it's a good idea to secure the towel with a wide elastic band, but don't fasten the elastic band too tightly. Leave the brush to dry naturally away from a direct heat source. When you remove the towel, the bristles will be straight, soft, and like new, ready for your next project.

HEALTH AND SAFETY

Some of the materials used for finishing wood are dangerous—indeed, many of them are poisonous, flammable, or corrosive—so always take care when using or handling them. Store materials safely, and make sure that waste is disposed of in the proper manner. Fire precautions must be taken at all times, and protective clothing worn in case of spillage. Common sense is good protection. Naked flames must never be permitted in the vicinity of flammable substances, and food or drink must never be consumed when there are poisonous materials around.

PROTECTIVE CLOTHING AND EQUIPMENT

Hands are the most frequent victims of chemicals. When using caustic strippers always wear heavy-duty elbow-length industrial gloves, otherwise ordinary PVC gloves are satisfactory. Household rubber gloves can be used for French polishing.

Whenever working with chemicals or in a dusty environment, wear safety goggles to protect your eyes from splashes or irritation. Alternatively, you can use a visor-type face guard, which you may find more comfortable than goggles.

To prevent inhalation of fumes and dust, there are simple masks or more complex battery-powered respirators, some of which have the advantage of incorporating eye protection and filtration (the latter is important when carrying out heavy sanding). A simple mask will suit most purposes.

Wearing overalls reduces the risk of dust, hairs, and fibers being transferred from clothing onto the surface of the work during finishing. When spraying, an overall that has a hood protects your hair from spray. A PVC apron must be worn when working with bleaches, strippers, and other chemicals—a cloth apron can be burnt by chemicals and, if that happens, the material may keep burning substances in close contact with your skin.

Noise can be injurious, too. Hearing protection is therefore essential when working with heavy machinery. The best kind of ear protectors are the ones that look like earphones. However, it is not always easy to wear them with goggles and a respirator, in which case, earplugs are a serviceable, if less effective, substitute. Clean earplugs regularly and keep them in a sealed box when you are not using them.

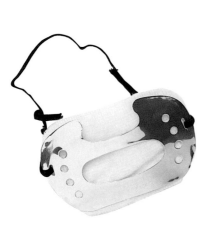

FLAT RESPIRATOR
This type of mask has a filter made of gauze that can be thrown away after use.

CUPPED DUST MASK
Supplied in packs and useful when sanding, this mask has a nose clip that fastens over the nose to prevent dust being inhaled.

FILTERED RESPIRATOR
A full-face respirator with changeable filter. Use while spraying or sanding to prevent dust and fumes being inhaled.

STORING MATERIALS

Caustic materials must be stored in a locked cabinet when not being used. Always keep the materials in the container they were supplied in, and make sure the label does not become detached. If it is necessary to decant caustic material, pour it carefully into a noncorrosive container made of glass, plastic, or earthenware. If any of the decanted material is left over, do not return it to its original container. Always wear gloves when handling caustic substances.

Flammable materials must be stored in a fireproof metal cabinet or a fireproof bin with a lid on it. Storage bins and cabinets need to be kept locked and must display a notice warning that the contents are flammable.

Labeling containers clearly is an essential safety precaution, but remember that children too young to read may be mobile and inquisitive, and hungry or thirsty.

Finishes must never be stored in or decanted into a food container or anything that resembles one. Milk bottles, saucers, and ice-cream cartons mean food to adults as well as children—and it may be too late when someone realizes that the contents are not what he or she expected.

WASTE DISPOSAL

Waste materials can and often do retain caustic characteristics. Correct disposal is therefore vital. Do not pour or throw chemicals or finishing materials down the drain—instead, find out from the appropriate authority where and how it is permissible to dispose of them.

LABELING

Do not remove manufacturers' labels from containers. They provide important information and warnings. It is worth dating finishes and other materials for future reference, as some have a finite shelf life and it is safest not to use materials that are past the specified date.

DUST AND FUMES

Most people realize that fumes are dangerous, but dust should not be underestimated as a health hazard, especially if you or your family suffer from hay fever, asthma, or other respiratory diseases. Also, it has been established that wood dust can cause nasal cancer, though the incidence of the disease is primarily among people exposed to large quantities. Many of the finishes and strippers that include hydrocarbon solvents can cause dizziness, which may lead to workshop accidents. It therefore makes sense to get into the habit of wearing a mask or respirator when spraying and sanding.

Before buying a filter for a mask or a respirator, read the recommended uses on the packaging to make sure it will provide effective protection against fine dust and harmful fumes. Some filters are designed to catch coarse dust particles only, and are not adequate for constant use.

FIRE PRECAUTIONS

Large quantities of chemicals and other combustible materials have to be stored in a brick building that has a retaining wall. A notice warning of the fire hazard must be prominently displayed on the exterior of the building. If you need more detailed information about regulations concerning flammable materials or about fire protection, contact the fire service, who will be glad to advise.

For effective fire prevention, position fire blankets, extinguishers, and fire buckets filled with sand (for dealing with spillages) around the workshop. A good-quality fire extinguisher that can cope with the relevant categories of fire is essential. Display a NO SMOKING sign and fit a smoke detector (or more than one in a large workshop).

Always keep the workshop as clean as possible. Dust constitutes a fire hazard, and in the event of an explosion in the workshop, fine dust is likely to be whipped out of nooks and crannies and blown around in clouds that can easily ignite. Secondary explosions caused by dust clouds can inflict greater damage and worse burns than the initial blast.

Even seemingly harmless substances can be potentially dangerous. Linseed oil, for example, dries by oxidation, which can cause a piece of cloth to heat and spontaneously ignite. Never throw rolled-up cloths soaked in linseed oil into a waste bin; instead, put them in a bucket of water, then dispose of them safely. If they are not being used for the moment but may be needed for further work, unroll them and allow them to dry outdoors.

Two-part finishes also present a fire hazard, since they heat up during the curing process, and should always be used with care.

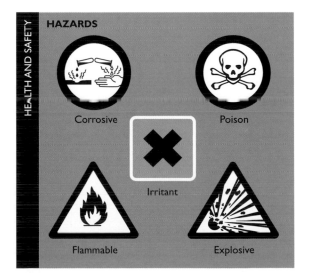

HEALTH AND SAFETY

HAZARDS

Corrosive

Poison

Irritant

Flammable

Explosive

GUIDE TO WOOD

The aim of finishing is to bring out the best in wood, enhancing the grain and color, while protecting the surface. It is therefore important to understand wood, and learn to identify the most common species. With that knowledge you will be able to apply the most appropriate finish for any particular type of wood.

Timbers are customarily divided into two groups, hardwoods and softwoods. This classification has a botanical basis. Softwoods have narrow leaves, whereas hardwoods have broad leaves. There is also a difference in wood structure between the two groups. From the woodworking point of view, hardwoods are generally denser and harder than softwoods. However there are exceptions. Balsa (Ochroma), for example, which is classified as a hardwood, is one of the lightest and softest woods there is.

PINE AND SIMILAR WOODS

Most pines *(Pinus spp)* and similar softwoods such as firs *(Abies spp)* and spruces *(Picea spp)* originate in the northern hemisphere, though some species come from elsewhere—for example, parana pine *(Araucaria angustifolia)* is native to South America. These woods grow quickly and, with proper forestry management, can be easily replaced. The lumbers are widely employed in building and joinery, and are being used more and more in the production of furniture. They can be used in solid or veneer form, or as core timbers faced with hardwood veneers. With appropriate finishing it is possible to enhance and improve the appearance of these woods.

The commercial timbers have a variety of names that do not always reflect their botanical origin. In fact, sometimes timber sold under a particular name may come from more than one species.

Always check softwood veneers for glue percolation, which can cause problems, and make sure any glue marks are removed before finishing. Since glue is often light in color, like the timber, it tends to be difficult to see. The best way to detect glue marks is to look across the surface to see them against the light.

Because pine and similar timbers tend to be soft, a tough good-quality finish is recommended when they are used for tabletops. Matte polyurethane finishes are suitable for this purpose.

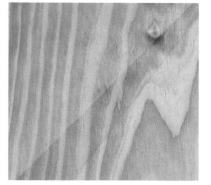

Southern yellow pine *(Pinus palustris)* is grown across the southern United States. The lumbers in this group are sold under a variety of names, including yellow pine, longleaf pine, and pitch pine. They are generally pale yellow to pale brown, but stains do not penetrate the resinous streaks present in the timber, so color matching is often needed. Natural-looking wax or thin matte finishes are recommended. An abraded matte finish looks attractive on these woods.

Lumbers sold as **"white pine"** *(Pinus strobus, Pinus monticola, Picea abies, Podocarpus dacrydioides)* have a fine grain and can be finished with tinted sealers or polishes to resemble mahogany. They are used for joinery and for painted or pigmented finishes. Always apply thin coats and rub completely flat, with fine (320 grit) abrasive paper to avoid leaving scratch marks as the wood is very soft. Two-part finishes can be used for greater protection.

Scots pine (*Pinus sylvestris*), also referred to as European redwood or red pine, is light colored with a distinctive figure and reddish or yellowish grain pattern. Scots pine is used for interior and exterior joinery, and for inexpensive pine furniture. It can be stained and takes finishes well, including wax and thin matte finishes. Waterborne finishes are good for producing a natural look.

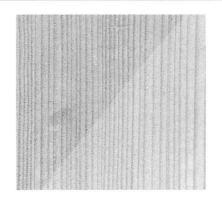

European spruce (*Picea abies*), also known as white deal, common spruce, or Norway spruce is used mainly for interior purposes because it is not sufficiently durable for outdoor use. It has a distinct grain pattern, with areas of light brown contrasting with the basic white color. The wood tends to look patchy when stained, due to uneven absorption. However, this can be overcome by using tinted sealers or polishes. Looks best with a thin satin or matte finish.

Sitka spruce (*Picea sitchensis*) is a good multi-purpose softwood, which has a natural springiness. It can be stained, but is better finished naturally because staining tends to look patchy.

Parana pine (*Araucaria angustifolia*) is very dense for a softwood and is ideal for home improvers just getting into woodwork.

Douglas fir (*Pseudotsuga menziesii*), also known as British Columbian or Oregon pine, has a pronounced grain pattern and a reddish color. It takes oil stains well, but not water or chemical stains.

- The color of pine can range from white or yellow to shades of pink, and depends more on the species than on the climate. Light-colored varieties are ideal for painted finishes, since not many coats are needed to produce a white or pastel finish. Some species have a pronounced grain pattern produced by the growth rings.
- Preparation is important, as the grain structure varies considerably. Use fine grades of paper during final sanding. When cutting back coats of finish, always sand right back until it looks as if the finish has been removed. The smoother the surface, the better the finish. Before using two-part finishes, apply a barrier coat of shellac sealer.
- Timbers like pine can be stained with oil or water stains; alcohol stains tend to look patchy. Pigment-suspension stains may be used to simulate other woods, and can produce some interesting effects. Matte or satin finishes are recommended (high-gloss finishes tend not to look so good).
- If the wood has a bold grain, color matching may be necessary. Select a natural brown alcohol stain to bring out the character of the timber and apply with a soft cloth.
- Water-based finishes are often extremely effective on pines, producing a natural "unfinished" look to the wood.
- Bright colors such as red and blue can also be used, although it is wise to experiment first. In fact, it is always best before any kind of coloring to try out stains on a small scrap of the same timber.

BEECH

Beech *(Fagus spp)* is grown in Europe, North America, and Japan. Variations sometimes occur due to climate and growing conditions. With proper forestry control it is a sustainable timber. Beech is a hard, very versatile, close-grained wood with an even grain pattern. The color ranges from a whitish or pale brown to a darker reddish brown. When steamed, beech becomes pink.

The timber is used mainly for furniture—particularly chair frames, as it lends itself to bending or shaping and takes upholstery well. It is also suitable for turning, and is therefore often used for making turned legs, handles, and toys.

For use as a show wood, beech can be stained to imitate other timbers, such as mahogany, walnut, and oak, and can then be treated with gloss, matte, pigmented, or waterborne finishes.

FINISHES FOR BEECH

Because beech is a close-grained timber, grain fillers are not necessary. However, cross grain sometimes causes problems, in which case a cabinet scraper can be used during final sanding. If bleaching is needed to lighten the color of the wood, a two-part bleach gives the best results. Two or more applications may be necessary to bleach the timber white.

Natural beech is attractive in its own right, although pigmented stains can be used to obtain an evenly colored finish or to provide a range of colors, including blue, red, and traditional brown. When attempting to match colors using modern finishes, spray tints are useful because they enable you to achieve a very accurate match.

Although beech stains well, oil wood dyes can bite into it, causing a dark effect in the grain. End grain should be sealed with thinned shellac to prevent stain penetrating too deeply and darkening the wood too much.

American beech *(Fagus grandifolia)* is easy to work, consistent, and inexpensive. However, it is not especially decorative, so is often finished with paint or stain, which it takes well.

European beech *(Fagus sylvatica)* is very similar to its North American cousin.

Medullary rays, which appear as tiny dark flecks, are a distinguishing feature in quarter-sawn boards.

BIRCH AND SIMILAR WOODS

A close-grained hardwood, birch *(Betula spp)* is native to both Europe and North America. The grain can be straight or swirling, or an attractive "water-grain" pattern. The heartwood is reddish yellow, and the sapwood white. Birch is used for furniture, paneling, and the production of plywood. It is sometimes finished to imitate other timbers.

FINISHES FOR BIRCH

Because the grain grows in both directions, careful preparation is needed.

Birch lends itself to natural finishes. It has an extremely close texture, so very few coats of finish are required.

HINTS AND TIPS

The grain pattern of birch tends to affect the absorption of stain, resulting in uneven color. Before you stain a piece, it is therefore advisable to test the effect on an inconspicuous area or a scrap piece of the same wood.

Most species have some form of figuring, but in birch it is indistinct. It does, however, give it a little more depth.

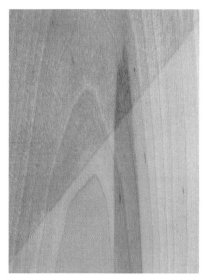

European birch *(Betula pendula)* tends to have an uninteresting pattern and color, but it takes stain well. It is used mostly for utility purposes.

European sycamore *(Acer pseudoplatanus)*, like birch, is a white lumber (though it has a slight flash in the figure) and can be finished in a similar way.

Birch is one of North America's most prolific species. **Yellow birch** *(Betula alleghaniesis)* is the most readily available and the best for woodworkers. It takes stain well.

OAK

Oak *(Quercus spp)* has been used by man for hundreds of years for many different purposes and in all sorts of places, ranging from churches, stately homes, and castles to boats and ships. It is a tough, hard-wearing timber, with excellent woodworking properties.

There are reputed to be over 200 different types of oak, which divide into two main groups—red oak and white oak. The white oaks are considered superior to the red, as they have a finer texture. Within this basic subdivision, differences occur due to variation in growth and climate.

FINISHES FOR OAK

Oak lends itself to thin semi-gloss or matte finishes, and responds particularly well to waxing. It is often pickled. Other open-grained timbers, such as ash and elm, can be finished in a similar way to oak.

A number of different terms for oak finishes are used in the wood-finishing trade—such as church oak, Flemish oak, and mission oak. Treat these names with caution, as they mean different finishes to different people.

When using red oak, the red tint can be overcome by applying a weak wash of green alcohol stain before proceeding with any other finish.

More than a third of the timber produced in the United States is oak. Most of this oak is **red** *(Quercus rubra)* (above left), although **white oak** *(Quercus alba)* (above right) is grown too. American red oak is much underestimated, and with the right treatment can produce some attractive effects.

European oak *(Quercus robur)* is the hardest of the oaks, and therefore tends to be harder to work. It is generally preferred for furniture making.

When quarter-sawn, both **white oak** (above) and **red oak** (above right) show medullary rays running across the grain pattern.

MAPLE

Maple *(Acer spp)* is a native of North America. Its uses vary from furniture to flooring, and the color ranges from white to light brown. Two varieties of maple are available as commercial timber. Hard maple (also known as sugar maple) is the harder of the two. Soft maple (also known as red maple) is not, in reality, that much softer than hard maple. It has a darker color and is much easier to work.

FINISHES FOR MAPLE

Because of its close grain, maple takes most finishes well. It can be treated with either a matte or gloss finish, as required. A grain filler is not needed.

HINTS AND TIPS

Staining maple with mahogany crystals produces a finish resembling cherry. Other stains can be used, but maple has a good natural color that needs no improvement.

If using two-part acid-catalyst finishes, apply a shellac or sanding sealer first, as the acid tends to redden the timber.

Hard maple *(Acer saccharum)* is popular for furniture making and interior fittings, particularly kitchens and flooring. Wax does not sink into the grain, but it will take polish or varnish.

Soft maple *(Acer rubrum)* has a more interesting color and grain pattern than hard maple and generally finishes well.

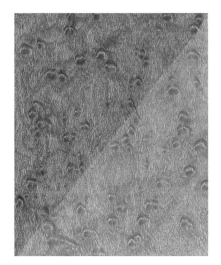

Bird's-eye maple makes a highly decorative veneer and is produced when growth buds form but fail to penetrate the bark. As a result, when the timber is cut, an attractive grain pattern, looking rather like watered silk, is revealed.

Burls come from growths that form on trees, caused by the loss of a branch or a wound to the bark. Affecting only part of a tree, burls are valuable and are often sliced for veneer. The patterning in a **maple burl** is one of the most dramatic.

MAHOGANY

Mahoganies (*Swietenia* spp, *Khaya* spp, *Melia* spp) come from several parts of the world—including the West Indies, Central and South America, South-East Asia, and West Africa. The characteristics, which depend on the timber's origin, range from the hard, heavy mahogany grown in Cuba to the much softer wood found in Nigeria and other parts of West Africa.

Mahogany is a favorite wood for pianos, and the deep red variety used for the backs of guitars, violins, and other stringed instruments is known as "fiddleback mahogany." Recently, American mahogany has become particularly popular; the color varies from golden brown to pale pink.

FINISHES FOR MAHOGANY

Mahogany has a rich color and figure that is second to none, so should be finished using as little surface coloring as possible. Many furniture manufacturers use coats of color unnecessarily, masking the natural figure and color of the wood.

Originally mahogany furniture was waxed or oiled, but in Victorian times French polishing became more fashionable.

When staining mahogany, avoid reddening the color too much—it is better to aim for a brown tone. As mahogany is an endangered timber, it should not be used indiscriminately. Instead, you can stain butternut (see page 22) to a mahogany shade, using mahogany crystals dissolved in water

Cuban mahogany (*Swietenia mahogani*) is loved for its texture, color, and patterning, but due to overexploitation, is now all but extinct. Recycling old furniture is the only ethical way to work with this wood.

American mahogany (*Swietenia macrophylla*) is just about the only true mahogany still commercially available. It has the pink color of Cuban mahogany, but the texture and pattern is less consistent.

African mahogany (*Khaya ivorensis*) is the color of genuine mahogany, but is one of the poorest of the species.

Sometimes confused with medullary rays, figuring describes the shimmering bands or streaks that usually run at right angles to the grain. In mahogany, as shown here in **American mahogany**, figuring tends to be inconsistent and concentrated.

As the tree grows taller, the larger branches twist and the fibers pull against each other. This produces the most highly figured mahogany. The "crotch" is the fork formed where the branches stem from the trunk. This is **Crotch African mahogany.**

TEAK

Teak *(Tectona grandis)* is a hard timber with good weathering properties. It is grown in Burma, India, Thailand, Malaysia, and Zambia. The natural color ranges from a golden yellow to a darker brown. Being naturally oily, it is suitable for decking on boats and other situations exposed to moisture. However, the oily nature of teak can cause problems for the finisher, such as poor adhesion, bubbling, and, with some two-part finishes, curling.

Before treating teak with any type of finish, other than an oil-based one, it is advisable to apply a shellac sealer.

A thin matte finish displays the timber's natural characteristics to best advantage.

The traditional way of finishing teak was to use several coats of linseed oil. Today, finishes such as teak or Danish and tung oils are available. These dry faster than linseed oil, are easier to apply, and provide a more durable finish. Alternatively, for a fine semi-gloss finish, you can treat teak with a polyurethane oil.

It is possible to use stains on teak, but they do not take well. When applying water stains, add 1 teaspoon of ammonia to 1 pt (0. 5 l).

Use thin coats when finishing teak. A matte or satin finish is best.

For outside use, treat teak with an exterior-grade varnish.

Teak is a beautiful and durable hardwood, but it is not known for its patterning. However, a quarter sawn surface often shows attractive dark lines at irregular intervals.

Teak, a first choice for boat building and outdoor furniture, has been exploited for centuries and is now largely only available from plantations and is costly to purchase.

Teak is well suited to making beautiful and durable outdoor furniture such as this garden bench.

WALNUT AND SIMILAR WOODS

The color of walnut (*Juglans spp*) can range from a dark, almost black, heartwood to a pale gray sapwood. It is possible to bleach the timber to a creamy color (blonde walnut was all the rage in the 1920s and 1930s), which gives it a rather washed-out appearance. As walnut has such strength, it can be fashioned into attractive shapes—for example, highly figured chair frames, with the grain running through.

FINISHES FOR WALNUT

Because of the natural beauty of the wood, the traditional finish for walnut was a wax one. Indeed, since walnut has so many natural colors and attractive grain patterns, there is a feeling among finish designers and woodworkers that these should be preserved by using either semi-gloss or matte waxed or oiled finishes. However, although it is considered that a gloss finish detracts from the timber's appearance, it is sometimes necessary and can look just as attractive as a matte treatment.

Black walnut (*Juglans nigra*) is grown widely across North America (and is often referred to as American walnut) and has a distinctive black grain. It is a strong wood, which feels surprisingly lightweight for a hardwood.

English walnut (*Juglans regia*), also known as European walnut, has a strong dark figure and a fine grayish color, with the dark streaks that are characteristic of walnut. It is now in short supply and, therefore, very expensive.

Walnut is often used in veneer form. Burl veneer (also known as burr veneer) is formed where there are outgrowths from the trunk, which have intricately grained timber. **European walnut burl** (left) produces a beautiful veneer, with a series of close-spaced oysters. **Black walnut burl** (right) is less dramatic, but has a more even color.

Butternut (*Juglans cinera*) grows along the east coast of North America and shares the texture, weight, and grain of black walnut, but is much paler.

ASH

Ash *(Fraxinus spp)* is a strong hardwood with a distinctive grain. It is pale in color and renowned for its flexibility. Its bendability lends itself well to furniture making, interior joinery, and boat building, as well as specialist uses such as umbrella handles. It is an excellent wood to turn and its good shock resistance makes it an ideal wood for tool handles and sports equipment. Ash thrives throughout North America, Europe, and Japan and is readily available.

FINISHES FOR ASH

- Ash has a coarse, straight, open grain and will take most finishes and stains well. However, this wood can have hard patches which may not take stain well, creating interesting effects.
- For a polished finish you may need to use grain filler and you should sand carefully to eliminate cross-grain scratching, particularly if you are using a dark stain.
- Like other open-grained woods, ash's open grain lends itself to pickling. The result is effective because most of the color remains in the large pores and accents the overall appearance of the grain.

HINTS AND TIPS

The color of ash can vary from a reddish tinged brown (white ash) to creamy pale brown (European ash) to dark brown (olive ash). Ash also tends to yellow with age.

White ash *(Fraxinus americana)* is open grained and its open pores show up even when stained. It easy to find and relatively cheap for a hardwood.

European ash *(Fraxinus excelsior)* also has a distinctive grain pattern and few defects, with open pores that show up even when stained.

European ash is prone to fungal disease and logs sometimes turn dark brown, causing dramatic effect. This wood is sold as **olive ash** and is much sought after.

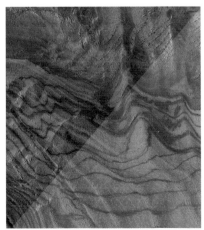

This combination of a burl with a disease creates a stunning effect, with brown lines of olive ash blending with the wild grain and quilting of the burl.

01

PREPARATION

To achieve satisfactory results it is imperative that a wood surface is adequately prepared before a finish is applied. Blemishes must be smoothed away, marks cleaned, and holes filled. A smooth and clean surface is essential, as any blemish will be exaggerated by the finish. Use fingers and eyes to check for faults assiduously—but you will soon be able to judge instinctively whether a surface has been adequately prepared. Take time and care over this stage to produce a surface fit for finishing.

TOOLS AND EQUIPMENT

Although one attraction of finishing is the limited selection of
tools required, experienced finishers will have built up a sizable
toolkit. Novice finishers may not need a wide range of tools, but
certain items, which may not at first seem obvious, are essential
aids to successful finishing.

Shown here is a basic toolkit for the preparation
of surfaces prior to finishing.

Cabinet scrapers
Cabinet scrapers are used by skilled
craftsmen to take off the finest of shavings.
The beginner should practice using cabinet
scrapers on a spare piece of wood.

G-clamp
Do not be tempted
to buy a large and
unwieldy clamp. A
4-inch clamp is fine.

Small hand drill
A drill is useful when
hammering in molding
and pane pins that may
split the timber.

Steel wool
You will need steel
wool in different
grades, from coarse
to fine. Always wear
protective gloves
when working with
steel wool, as the
fibers are sharp.

Scalpel
A scalpel is vital for
cutting and can also
be used for scraping
unwanted finish.

Stopping knife
Tailor-made for applying wood fillers. Do not let the filler dry on the knife.

Wire brushes
Useful for opening up the grain when applying a limed finish, and for stripping moldings and carvings.

Chisels
Chisels are handy for cleaning off glue when working on old pieces.

Synthetic-bristle brush
Made from vegetable fibers, these are ideal for bleaching.

Gooseneck scraper
A development of the cabinet scraper is the molding or gooseneck scraper, found in a variety of shapes, combining profiles and radii.

Sanding machine
An important feature of any sander is a good dust-extraction system to minimize scratching.

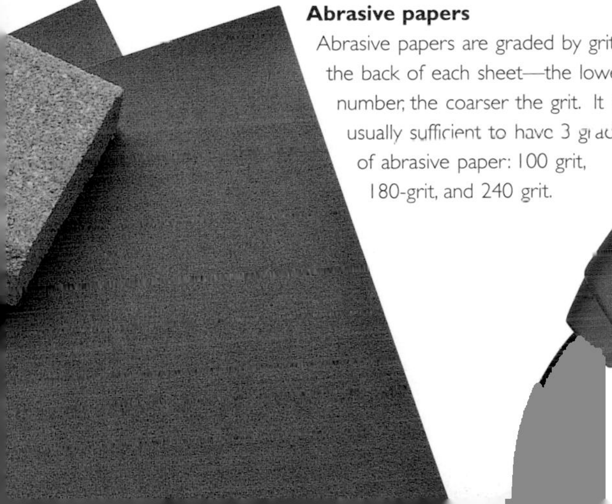

Sanding block
Use a sanding block to ensure an even distribution of pressure when sanding.

Abrasive papers
Abrasive papers are graded by grit size on the back of each sheet—the lower the number, the coarser the grit. It is usually sufficient to have 3 grades of abrasive paper: 100 grit, 180-grit, and 240 grit.

18mm

25mm

BOSCH
PSS 23 A
150 W · 92 x 230 mm · 20,000/min

SEE ALSO
Using solvent strippers, pages 34–37
Restoration, pages 52–55

28

PREPARATION

IDENTIFYING EXISTING FINISHES

Before cleaning or embarking on any restoration or polishing work, try to identify the finish. This is not always easy. Something about the finish can be deduced from the age of a piece, but previous restorations and renovations may have replaced the original finish with a more modern version.

YOU WILL NEED

Protective gloves
Cotton cloth
Denatured alcohol
Sharp blade

CURLS

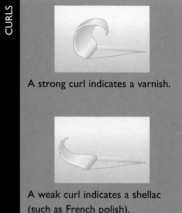

A strong curl indicates a varnish.

A weak curl indicates a shellac (such as French polish).

A powder indicates a synthetic material.

For example, French polish was the first durable finish to be widely used. Previous finishes, oil and wax, needed regular maintenance to keep their appearance, and during the nineteenth century they were often replaced with a French-polished finish. Oil and wax finishes found favor again in the late nineteenth and early twentieth centuries on Arts and Crafts furniture, and these finishes often still survive today.

By the mid twentieth century, French polish had generally been superseded by spray lacquers, owing to considerations of cost and ease of application.

For a thorough identification, test a small area, if possible on a hidden part of the piece, such as the underside of a table or the back of a rail.

01 Wearing protective gloves, charge a swab or pad of cotton cloth with denatured alcohol.

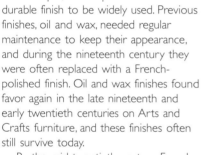

02 Apply the swab or pad to the surface and rub in a circular motion for two minutes. After this time, if the surface becomes sticky, the indication is that you have a reversible finish, such as shellac or shellac varnish. If the surface treatment does not soften, the indication is that you are dealing with a nonreversible finish.

03 Scratch the softened surface treatment with a sharp blade so that the material comes off in a curl (see Curls, above).

OIL FINISH

Characteristic appearance

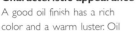

A good oil finish has a rich color and a warm luster. Oil brings out the color of the timber but unless it has been maintained it may look flat and dry, as the finish will have been absorbed into the timber.

The test Moisten your finger with a little white spirit and apply to a concealed part of the item. Although the surface may look quite dry, the presence of an oil finish may prevent the white spirit from further darkening its color.

WAX FINISH

Characteristic appearance A good wax finish has a satin sheen with a "low build"—that is, the grain will not be full and the surface will not be glossy. However, an old wax finish may appear flat and dull.

The test Moisten your finger with a little white spirit and rub it on a concealed part of the item. A wax finish will feel sticky and start to come away on your finger.

FRENCH POLISH

Characteristic appearance

A good French-polished finish will have a "high build," completely filling the grain and presenting a bright, full-bodied surface. French polish is most often found on pianos (made before 1950) and decorative furniture.

The test Test an inconspicuous part with a little methylated spirit. Rub the surface with a moistened finger and if the finish is French polish, it will slowly become sticky and soft.

SPRAY LACQUERED FINISH

Characteristic appearance

Usually much harder than French polish, spray lacquer is often colored and applied to unstained timber. This can often obscure the grain a little and give a very uniform color and glow over the whole item. The finish is usually bright and glossy, although some lacquers do contain a dulling agent.

The test Look for damaged areas. Chips in the finish reveal white unstained timber. Hard lacquers can be prone to cracking.

SANDING AND SCRAPING

Sanding not only smooths the surface of the wood but also prepares it for subsequent treatments and finishes. The term "sandpaper" is commonly used to describe any type of abrasive grit on flexible backing sheets. These days, the grit is rarely sand, or even glass, as all sorts of materials are now used for abrading wood. There is also a variety of backings available, to suit different types of work, including those made from cloth, card, and Velcro. It is worth investigating the various options.

HEALTH AND SAFETY

It is a good idea to wear a dust mask or respirator when sanding, especially if you are sanding a lot of material.

ABRASIVE PAPERS

Abrasives are graded by grit size—the lower the number, the coarser the grade. You will rarely need abrasive coarser than 80 grit, and 240 grit is usually fine enough for preparing surfaces. You may want to use a finer grade between coats, but note that when machine-sanding, the speed of the abrasive over the surface makes each grade more powerful than when sanding by hand.

Woodworkers and finishers often talk about "working through the grades," referring to the technique of using a series of grit grades, progressing from coarse to fine, when preparing a piece. Three steps are normally enough—starting with 100 grit, then changing to 180 grit, and finishing with 240 grit. These descriptions of grit grades are not always standard, so look out for alternative methods of grading when selecting abrasives.

GARNET

Garnet is the most common general-purpose abrasive. It is often worth rubbing garnet paper on a scrap piece of metal before using it for finishing, because the grit is sharp and can carve out deep scratches. Garnet paper is best used by hand, as the bond is not strong enough to survive machine-sanding.

ALUMINUM OXIDE

Aluminum oxide is the man-made alternative to garnet. It is supplied on a variety of backings and can be used by hand and for machine-sanding. Its open coat of abrasive allows rapid stock removal with little clogging. Cloth-backed aluminum oxide has a longer life and is more flexible than many paper-backed grades. Use the cloth-backed versions when sanding with machines.

SILICON CARBIDE

While silicon carbide is an abrasive paper, it is not suitable for preparation work. Instead it is used when rubbing back between coats of finish, when it is important to reduce scratching. This modern alternative to using soap and water or mineral spirits when rubbing between coats has a powder substance filling the gaps between the abrasive grains, thus reducing the likelihood of clogging and scratching. It works well for hand and machine-sanding.

Below (from left to right); three grades of silicon-carbide paper; four grades of Webrax, non-woven nylon fibers. On top left is a sanding file with spare paper; top of right is sanding string.

PRO TIP

PREPARATION
If you need to raise the grain, wet the wood and allow it to dry before sanding

HINTS AND TIPS

- You can cut up abrasive sheets with scissors or by folding and tearing. One recommended technique is to cut sheets into quarters. Do not simply fold sheets in four, because the abrasive coats will then be facing each other and are likely to wear more quickly.
- Use a block, made of cork, wood, or rubber when sanding flat surfaces.
- Maintain an even pressure when sanding by hand.
- Convex or concave blocks (as appropriate) make sanding curved surfaces easier and more efficient.
- If the abrasive is too sharp, take off the first edge by rubbing it on scrap wood or metal.
- Tap abrasive paper on the back when it becomes clogged with dust.
- Check the surface of the wood frequently by using an oblique light source to show up imperfections.
- Use fingers to check the finish they are often better than eyes.

SANDING YOUR SURFACE

When using abrasive paper start with a coarse grade and working down through to the finer grades, dusting away the debris with a tack cloth after each sanding. Using a sanding block is the easiest technique: a cork block is ideal because the edges are softer than wood and are less likely to indent the surface you are sanding.

Once any existing surface finish has been removed (see pages 34–37), use a soft, wet cloth to soak the surface of the wood and raise the grain ready for sanding.

Prepare sheets of 100-grit, 180-grit, and 210-grit abrasive papers by folding and cutting them to the size of your sanding block.

Wrap a piece of the coarsest (100-grit) abrasive paper around the sanding block. Using a sanding block is easier on the hand than sanding with the paper flat because the pressure is more evenly distributed, and ensures an even surface.

After sanding with abrasive paper, remove the dust and debris with a tack rag. Repeat Steps 3–4 using first a medium-grit, and then a fine-grit paper.

Different styles of sanding block are available: choose one that fits your hand and is comfortable to use.

To sand around curves and rounded forms like table or chair legs, run a strip of abrasive paper up and down at 90 degrees to the edge. Start with a coarse grain and move through to the finest grades of abrasive paper.

SCRAPERS

For a really professional and highly smoothed finish, a scraper is ideal. Scrapers are very useful tools and come in a range of shapes for dealing with curves and corners. Used properly, they will produce a much cleaner and smoother surface than abrasive papers because they do not leave scratches. Scrapers remove a very fine amount of wood from the surface of an object because its edge has a burr, and this needs to be maintained. Creating that burr is achieved with a file and burnisher, but care is needed to maintain a scraper in good working order, as it will only cut well if the edge is kept straight and square.

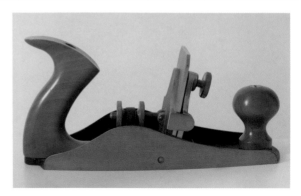

SCRAPER PLANE
The plane will hold the scraper blade firmly and at a constant angle, allows the steel to be worn down to the last, and fingers will not get burned!

USING A CABINET SCRAPER

To use a scraper, hold it in both hands, with your thumbs at the back, and push it across the surface, using long sweeping movements of even pressure along the grain of the wood. Alternatively, some people prefer to use a pulling action, with their fingers behind the scraper creating the pressure. The angle at which the scraper is held is determined by the angle of the burr. Experiment until thin shavings are produced. By pushing with your thumbs or fingers the scraper can be bent to aid the cut, with a tighter curve producing a narrower cutting area. However, take care not to remove too much material, as it is easy to produce furrows in the surface.

SPECIALIST SHARPENING TOOLS

You can buy specialist tools for putting burrs on the edge of cabinet scraper blades. The one pictured above allows you to set the angle of the burr required on a dial and then swipe the blade through the device, rather like swiping a credit card.

Once prepared, the cabinet scraper blade can be inserted into a holder. The burred edge will project from the holder.

The degree of curvature of the scraper blade can, on most holders, be adjusted by turning the central screw. Using both hands, hold the scraper at a slight angle away from you and push along the grain of the wood in straight movements.

The cabinet scraper blade can be used without a holder by holding the edges firmly and applying pressure with your thumbs to make a curve. Push the blade away from you along the grain of the wood in firm, smooth strokes.

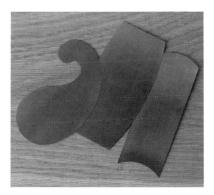

PAINT SCRAPERS
Other types of scraper, with handles, are available and are popular in the decorating trades—including, of course, paint scrapers.

MOLDING OR GOOSENECK SCRAPER
A development of the cabinet scraper is the molding or gooseneck scraper, found in a range of shapes, combining profiles, and radii.

CABINET SCRAPER
The cabinet scraper is the most commonly used scraper. In its simplest form it is a rectangle of steel, usually about 4 × 2 in. (100 x 50 mm), inserted into a holder.

SHARPENING A CABINET SCRAPER

01 Cut two thin blocks of wood, slightly larger than the scraper blade.

02 Make a "sandwich" of the blade between the two blocks of wood to stabilize the blade. The burred edge of the blade should project slightly beyond the edges of the blocks.

04 Using a burnisher or a knife-sharpening steel (as shown here), start at one end of the scraper blade and roll the burnisher or steel, using one complete diagonal stroke. The aim is to create an evenly burred edge of about five degrees along the whole blade's edge.

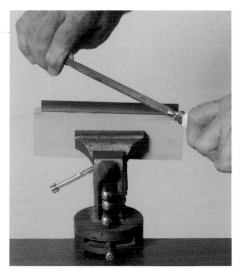

03 Secure the sandwich firmly in a vise. Using a medium flat file, "top off" the edge of the scraper by running the file flat against its edge. This ensures that the edge of the scraper blade is completely straight and true.

SEE ALSO
Health and safety, page 12
Identifying existing finishes, page 28
Sanding and scraping, page 30

PREPARATION

USING SOLVENT STRIPPERS

The removal of old finishes can be a laborious task, but must be carried out properly if subsequent finishing is to be a success. It is essential to clean any evidence of previous decoration or protection from the grain. Otherwise, it will show up later.

Removing old paint and varnish from wood is a simple process using solvent strippers, but care must be taken at all times to protect your skin, eyes, and surrounding areas.

USEFUL INFORMATION

FINISHING
Always ensure that the surface has been either neutralized or wiped with mineral spirits, whichever is appropriate, before refinishing.

Using cabinet scrapers or sanding is an alternative to chemical stripping, but is much more time-consuming, and unlikely to produce a better result. In addition, sanding or scraping removes the patina that certain woods, such as mahogany, acquire on aging. Sanding will also not remove the residue of finish from open-grained woods, so it is often better to use a solvent paint remover.

An alternative is to take the piece to a specialist who has access to sandblasting facilities or a caustic dipping tank. Unfortunately, this latter technique often loosens joints in furniture and doors. Sandblasting works well for intricate pieces and carving; it needs no neutralizing and usually leaves the wood ready for refinishing. When doing the work yourself, the choice of stripper is determined by the workpiece and the original finish. It is easy to distinguish paint from wax, but other finishes are more difficult to identify (see page 28).

SOLVENT STRIPPERS

Solvent strippers are supplied ready-mixed. They contain a mixture of solvents, usually methylene chloride, with some wax to stop them evaporating, and are used to remove French polish, cellulose-based finishes, oil, and wax. It may be necessary to apply several coats of stripper before the bulk of the old coating is removed. Before further work on the surface, some solvent strippers need to be neutralized.

Always check on the product's label. Be warned that solvent strippers in paste form contain caustic soda and will cause many woods to darken. Always work in a well-ventilated space, away from naked flames, and follow the manufacturer's instructions regarding storing and disposing of cans.

STRIPPING PAINT

Painting is one of the simplest ways of preserving wood and adding color, but completely removing all traces of paint takes some effort. However, thorough removal is the only way to ensure that any finish you want to apply later will not be marred by the previous decoration.

YOU WILL NEED

Protective gloves and goggles
Solvent stripper
Glass container
Old paintbrush
Paint scraper
Newspaper
Manufacturer's recommended
    neutralizer (where necessary)

01

Wearing protective gloves and goggles and working in a well-ventilated space, decant a small amount of the paint remover into a glass container. Use an old or inexpensive paintbrush to apply a liberal coating of stripper to the surface of the object.

Following the manufacturer's recommendations regarding timing, and when the paint has begun to form blisters, start removing the stripper and old paint using the flat edge of a paint scraper, working along the grain. In corners and angles, use the pointed end of the scraper.

Depending on the thickness of the original paintwork, you may need to reapply the stripper. It's also likely that a second application will be needed in intricately shaped or carved areas.

You can be scraping the residue of old paint from one surface while the stripper gets to work on another area. Remember, the chemicals in "peels" of stripper mixed with the old paint will still be active, so it's a good idea to wrap the waste tightly in layers of newspaper and then discard them carefully.

Depending on the brand of stripper, you may need to neutralize the effect using either plain water or a solution of water and washing soda crystals. Follow the manufacturer's instructions on the can and in either case, keep wearing protective gloves to avoid any contact with the unneutralized wood surface.

HINTS AND TIPS

- When using strippers that make the finish bubble, dab on a second coat of stripper to flatten and burst the blisters in order to bring the stripper into contact with the surface again.
- It does not help to "paint" the stripper onto the surface—it is better to lay down the first coat and dab on subsequent coats.
- Make sure the stripper is removed from all nooks and crannies, corners, and covings. Otherwise, it will react with stains and finishes.
- Some strippers will "melt" acrylic, so remember to remove your wristwatch.

USING A HOT-AIR GUN

Chemical strippers can be expensive and they must be disposed of carefully because of the dangerous solvents they contain. Although the initial expenditure is high, if you have a number of objects to strip, a hot-air gun is a good and greener investment.

STRIPPING VARNISH

Removing old varnish from wood is a simple process using solvent strippers, but care must be taken at all times to protect your skin, eyes, and surrounding areas. Some strippers will "melt" acrylic, so remember to remove your wristwatch. Always work in a well-ventilated space, away from naked flames, and follow the manufacturer's instructions regarding storing and disposing of cans.

YOU WILL NEED

Protective gloves and goggles
Glass container
Old paintbrush
Paint scraper
Newspaper

HEALTH AND SAFETY

• Wear protective gloves and goggles at all times when using strippers.
• Wash strippers off skin immediately with water.
• Take care when opening cans of stripper—pressure can build up and force the liquid to spurt out.
• Only use strippers outdoors or in well-ventilated areas. Do not use them in a confined space.
• Solvents can cause dizziness.
• Scrape off residue onto an old newspaper for disposal.
• Some strippers are flammable, so do not smoke or light a naked flame near them.
• Make sure all stripper is removed before handling the workpiece.
• Wear a dust mask or respirator when using aerosol solvent strippers.

01

Varnish can be removed by "painting" on a solvent-based varnish remover. Wearing protective gloves and goggles and working in a well-ventilated space, decant a small amount of the stripper into a glass container. Using a small, inexpensive paintbrush, paint on the stripper, working on a small area of the wood at a time.

02

When the varnish begins to soften and lift from the surface of the wood, you can begin to drag the flat edge of a paint scraper across the surface, moving in the direction of the grain. You may have to repeat this process two or three times because modern varnishes can be difficult to remove completely. Wrap the waste tightly in layers of newspaper and then discard them carefully.

YOU WILL NEED

Protective gloves and goggles
Gel-form solvent stripper
Old paintbrush
Stainless steel pot scourer
Newspaper

USING GELS

01

In addition to liquid solvents, you can also buy varnish stripper in gel form. These are useful in that they stick to the surface of the wood, which makes them ideal for use on vertical surfaces.

02

Gel strippers are removed from moldings and delicate edges with a stainless steel pot scourer. You may need several of these, replacing them as they become clogged. Dispose of them carefully.

USING AEROSOLS

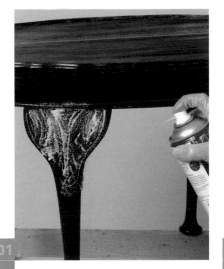

01

For fine moldings and in other areas where it might be difficult to paint on a solvent, aerosol strippers are available. You will need to wear a protective dust mask in order not to breathe in the fumes and fine spray, and you will need to mask off surrounding areas to protect them from overspray.

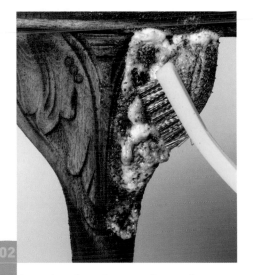

02

Once the solvent has reacted, use a fine copper wire brush to remove the old varnish. This is a good way of removing varnish from intricately shaped areas.

Once the old varnish has been removed, neutralize the stripper by washing the item in clean water and wiping dry.

YOU WILL NEED

Protective gloves, goggles, and dust mask
Aerosol solvent stripper
Fine copper wire brush
Cotton cloth

AFTER STRIPPING

Stripping can reveal many problems formerly concealed under years of paint. Some of the joints may be loose, and the piece may need some filling. If the piece is very badly scratched or dented, sand with progressively finer abrasive paper, starting with 100 grit and working up to 240. However, bear in mind that certain woods acquire a beautiful patina on aging that sanding would remove. Check the surface thoroughly for any remnants of finish, or any bruises and dents, before starting the next stages of restoration.

SEE ALSO
Sanding and scraping, page 30
Filling holes, page 40

PREPARATION

BRUISES, DENTS, AND SCRATCHES

Indentations in the surface are caused either by the compression of fibers (in the case of bruises and dents), or by the fibers being broken by scratches. These faults must be removed before sanding. If the bruises or scratches are deep, it is best to raise them rather than try to sand them out, since heavy sanding is likely to result in an uneven surface, and on a veneered piece it may even break through the veneer.

HINTS AND TIPS

- Excess water can be removed using the hot iron, but keep plenty of dry cloths available.
- Avoid direct contact between the iron and the workpiece, because there is always a risk of burning or further bruising.
- Take care when working on edges and moldings: these are easier to damage or burn than flat surfaces, and are often the most badly affected by faults.

YOU WILL NEED

Cotton cloth
Soldering iron (optional)
Iron
Fine abrasive paper
Tack rag

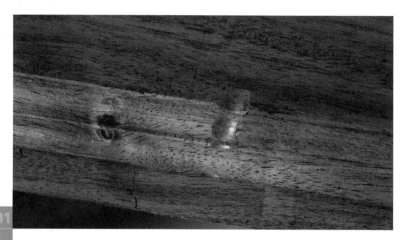

01 Dents, bruises, or scratches in beautiful furniture can be unsightly, but they can be removed without any specialist equipment, so that the piece is restored to its pristine condition. The principle of raising dents, bruises, or scratches is to swell the fibers of the timber by sweating with heat and steam. The expansion of the fibers levels the surface. This may not work fully when the fibers are badly broken, especially with deep scratches across the grain, but sweating will at least reduce the amount of filling or sanding needed.

02 Make sure that any old finish is thoroughly cleaned off the piece. Dampen the surface around the dent, bruise, or scratch with a cloth soaked in water. Always check that the water and cloth are clean—it is easy to discolor the wood. Using a soft, clean cloth soaked in clean water, gently moisten the area of the dent and its immediate surroundings. Press the cloth against the dent so that the water soaks into the fibers of the wood, and does not simply run off. Try not to wet too much of the piece.

APPROPRIATE SURFACES

Softwoods react faster than hardwoods to steaming. However, the differences in grain density are more prominent in softer timbers, so check that bruises have been raised thoroughly.

Steaming deep bruises works better on solid wood than on a veneered surface. With veneer, the glue film can act as a barrier to the steam, and the fibers of the substrate may not expand as effectively as with solid timber.

DRYING TIME

Bruises can be raised within seconds, but leave the surface to dry before further work.

FINISHING

Where the fibers have been broken, filling and sanding will be necessary.

When using a hot iron, arrange your working area carefully, ensuring it is not cluttered and that the iron can be placed out of harm's way.

03 Fold the still damp cloth and lay it over the dented area. Do not use cloth that is too thin, otherwise there is a risk of burning or bruising the piece further. If you have a soldering iron, heat it up and press it gently onto the cloth over the dent.

04 If you don't have a soldering iron, use the tip of a domestic iron. Make sure the iron is very hot—the steam should not be allowed to disperse before it has entered the wood. Be careful not to let the full foot of the iron plate touch the wood that is not covered by the wet cloth. Press down with the iron until the steam ceases. Remove the iron and cloth to inspect the dent. If it is still there, repeat the operation, soaking the cloth with water each time. Leave the surface to dry before further finishing.

05 Once the dent has been removed, rub the area that has been treated using a fine abrasive paper, sanding in the direction of the grain.

06 Once the surface has been sanded, remove any dust with a tack rag. The repaired area is now ready to be finished using suitable materials, such as a lacquer, varnish, or polish, to match the original finish.

07 The restored piece with the repair imperceptible.

SEE ALSO
Sanding and scraping, page 30
Coloring wood, page 48
French polishing, page 84

PREPARATION

FILLING HOLES

Fillers are used for filling larger indentations in wood. Fillers have to match the color of the piece, and require an elastic nature to cope with the movement of timber. It is best to avoid using fillers, if at all possible, because a good match is always difficult. However, for cracks, knots, and deep scratches there is often no alternative. Select the best filler for the situation. When choosing a filler, it is important to bear in mind the type of finish you intend to use on the piece.

Shellac sticks are suitable for any finish, but plastic wood (in either two- or one-part form) is difficult to match. If you intend to use a stain to do so, make sure it is compatible. The instructions will say whether it is oil- or water-based. As a general rule, use shellac fillers under traditional finishes, and two-part fillers under modern spray finishes. Only use wax fillers for small chips, and then only while polishing, or with a wax or oil finish. Plastic wood is most commonly used under varnishes.

WATER-BASED WOOD FILLERS

Water-based wood fillers can be thinned with water. They have the advantage of being quick-drying and suffer very little shrinkage. They are available in a wide range of colors and are cheaper than two-part fillers.

TWO-PART FILLERS

Two-part fillers are harder versions of plastic wood. A catalyst or hardener reacts with the filler to create a very strong repair. They are available in a variety of colors, and can be matched using stains and pigments. However, achieving an exact match can be difficult, so they are better used for structural repairs (especially on particle board) than for filling conspicuous faults. Follow the manufacturer's instructions carefully, leaving it slightly proud. Two-part fillers do shrink, but not to the extent of plastic wood, and they set very hard—so beware of overfilling, which will necessitate time-consuming chiseling and sanding later.

USEFUL INFORMATION

DRYING TIMES
- Plastic wood needs about 20 minutes to dry.
- Two-part fillers dry in about 30 minutes.
- Shellac sticks dry instantly.
- Glue and sawdust takes at least three hours.
- Wax sticks do not need any drying time.
- Pigment and white polish (shellac) used to color filler takes two to three minutes to dry.

HINTS AND TIPS

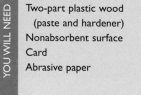
- Sprayed lacquers can dry unevenly on fillers.
- Plastic wood tends to fall out of large cavities.

YOU WILL NEED

Two-part plastic wood (paste and hardener)
Nonabsorbent surface
Card
Abrasive paper

01 Mix the hardener to the paste on a clean nonabsorbent surface. The usual mix is a golf-ball size piece of paste to a pea-size piece of hardener. Mix the two together well.

02 Using a piece of card, push the filler into the hole firmly and smooth off, leaving it just proud on the surface. Overfill will lead to time and effort wasted in sanding down smooth.

03 When dry, after about 20 minutes, sand off the filler level with the surrounding surface ready for painting or finishing.

PLASTIC WOOD

Available from most hardware stores, this commonly used filler comes in a tin and is made in a range of colors. It dries out quickly, so remember to replace the lid immediately after use.

Plastic wood does not always adhere effectively, so ensure any faults are clean and dust-free. Apply with a knife or chisel, pressing the filler well into the cavity. Plastic wood has a tendency to shrink, so leave proud to dry. It may even be necessary to use more than one application, so for large holes, fill gradually.

SHELLAC STICKS

Shellac sticks are sold in a variety of colors to suit a range of woods, and are a concentrated form of the shellac used for French polishing. They are available from only a few specialist hardware stores and by mail order. The shellac is melted into the fault using a soldering iron. Shellac filling should not be used under two-part cold-cure lacquers.

YOU WILL NEED

Shellac stick
Soldering iron
Scraper
240 grit abrasive
paper

01 Shellac sticks are available in a large range of colors and can be used to match most common woods.

02 Shellac sticks can be used to fill and smooth out a small hole or cavity and make it disappear. Match the shellac stick to the color of the wood surface. Heat up a soldering iron.

03 While holding the stick over the hole, touch it with the hot iron. The tip of the stick will melt and drop into the hole. Although you want the melted shellac to stand slightly proud in the repair, do not overdo it because the more shellac you use, the more you will have to remove.

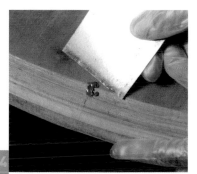

04 The shellac will harden in seconds. Use a tool such as a scraper or the back of a knife to remove the excess. Take care not to dig into the surrounding area.

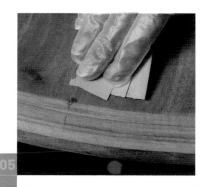

05 When you have removed as much of the excess shellac as you can with the scraper, use abrasive paper, about 240 grit, to smooth the remaining shellac still standing proud of the surface.

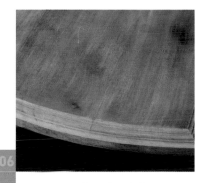

06 Continue sanding the shellac to a flat smooth surface level with the surrounding wood. You can now stain and finish the item.

WAX STICKS

Manufacturers of wax finishes also make sticks for small repairs. These are colored and designed for use either on surfaces to be waxed or on pieces already polished. Clear beeswax may be sufficient in many circumstances, especially when the hole is small. Wax must not be used under modern finishes.

YOU WILL NEED

Wax stick
Protective gloves
Plastic spatula
Cotton cloth

01 Wax sticks are available in a range of colors and can be used to match most common woods.

02 To use a wax filler on small cracks or holes, wearing protective gloves, take a small amount of wax from a stick and roll it between your fingers so that the heat makes it soft and malleable.

GLUE AND SAWDUST MIX

A quick and cheap filler can be made by mixing glue with sawdust to match the workpiece. It is not a good filler for large areas, and not all finishes take to it, but it does work well for gaps along joint lines.

When using PVA adhesive, mix it with sawdust produced by sanding either the piece to be repaired or an offcut of the original timber. PVA will not fill gaps, so plenty of wood dust is needed to act as a filler. Alternatively, for larger holes, mix sawdust with a urea-formaldehyde adhesive.

Leave all these mixtures slightly proud, then chisel and sand them flat when dry.

YOU WILL NEED

Card
Sawdust
PVA or urea-
    formaldehyde glue
Plastic spatula (optional)
Abrasive papers

01 On a piece of card, add the sawdust to the glue and mix with another piece of card until the mixture has a thick but workable consistency. The glue must be thoroughly mixed in to achieve a good bond.

02 Apply the filler with the mixing card or a plastic spatula. Spread it over the fault, building up to the surface until it is smooth but a little proud.

03 Leave the glue and sawdust filler for at least three hours to dry. It will then be stuck firmly into the hole, and hard enough to be shaped and smoothed with abrasive papers.

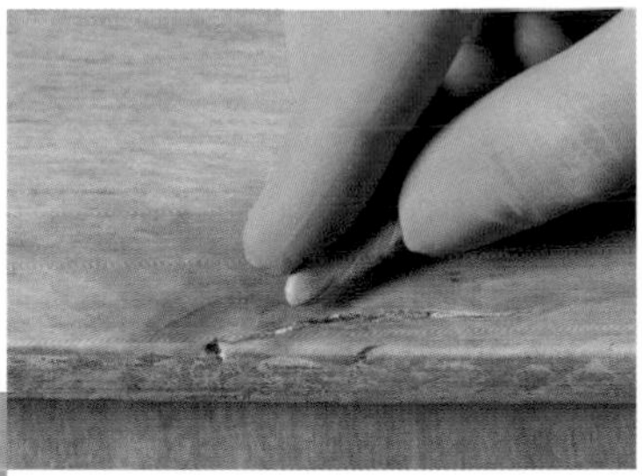

03

Press the soft wax into the crack or hole.

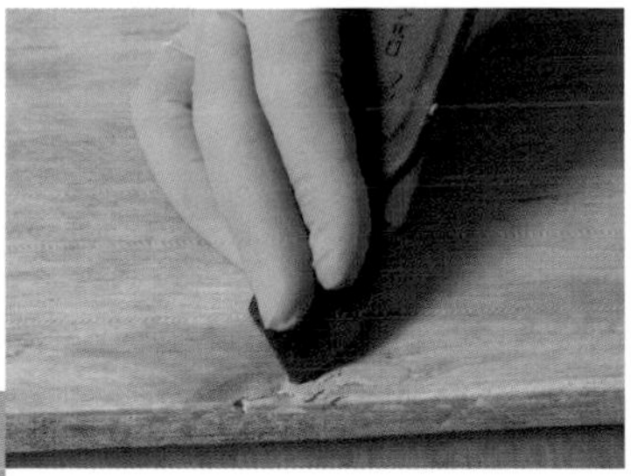

04

Using a spatula (plastic is preferred), press the wax into the crevice until it is compressed and smooth with the surface.

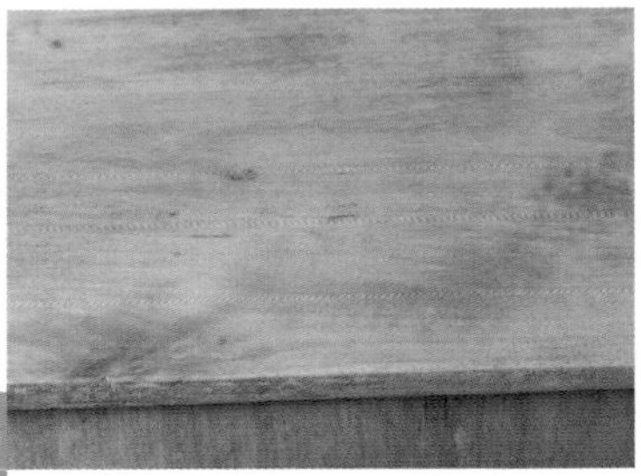

05

Finally, use a cotton cloth to buff up the area so that the wax filler does not show. You could add another coating of colored wax over the whole area to help the wax filler blend into its surroundings.

USING PIGMENTS TO COLOR FILLER

YOU WILL NEED

- Pigments
- White polish (shellac)
- Artists' brush
- Card
- Protective gloves

HINTS AND TIPS

- Apply the pigment in thin layers, building up the color as you go.
- Always make sure you work with good natural light when mixing and matching pigments.
- Wear gloves to protect your fingers from staining.

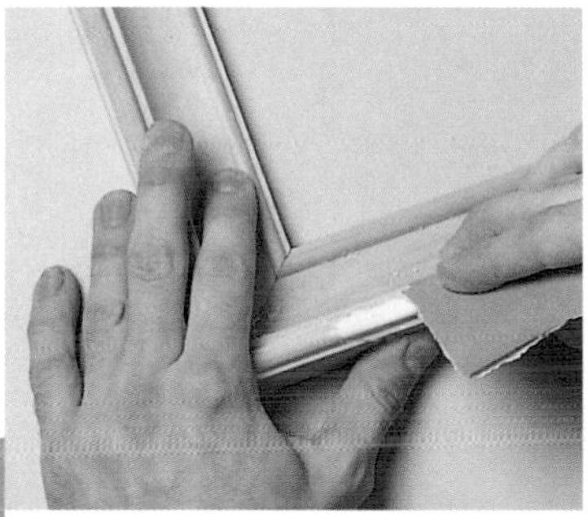

01

Once your filler is dry and has been sanded smooth, you can use pigments to match the repair with the rest of the surface of the piece. Pigments are opaque colors ground into a binding medium, which can be oil, acrylic, alkyd, or shellac.

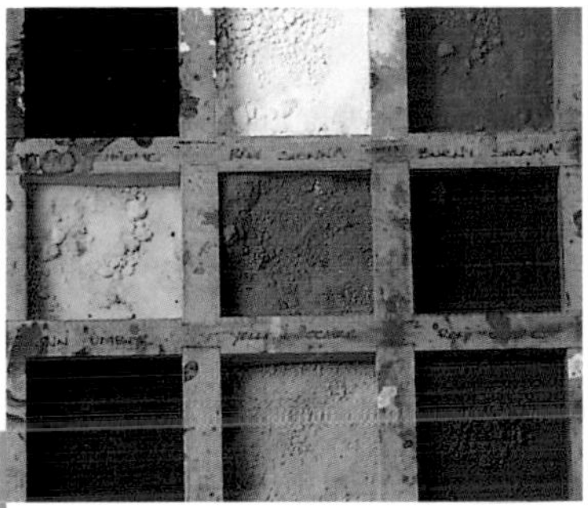

02

A selection of nine pigment colors is sufficient, stored in a segmented tray. Experiment with combinations of pigments to judge the color matches they produce. White polish (shellac) can be used as the binder over any of the fillers used here.

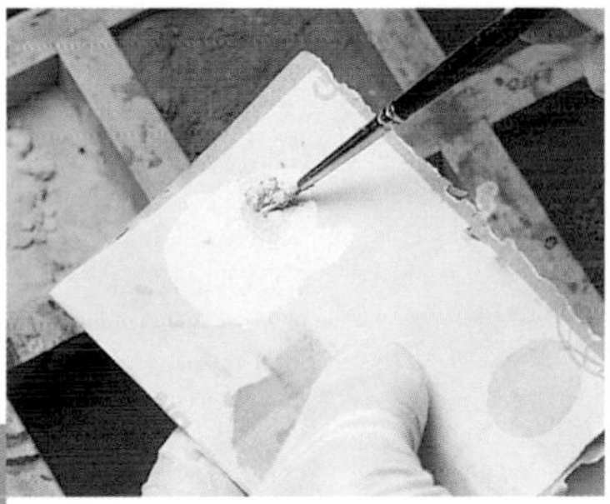

03

Mix the pigments with white polish and apply with an artists' brush. Dip the brush into the polish and then into the required pigment, and mix. Here titanium white and yellow ocher are being mixed to produce a light color.

04

Apply the mixture of pigment and polish with the artists' brush, stroking on the color and imitating the grain pattern. Blend in the color gradually. Leave to dry for two to three minutes. Gradually apply more white polish over the filler to bring out the color, but bear in mind that too much polish at a time will rub off the color.

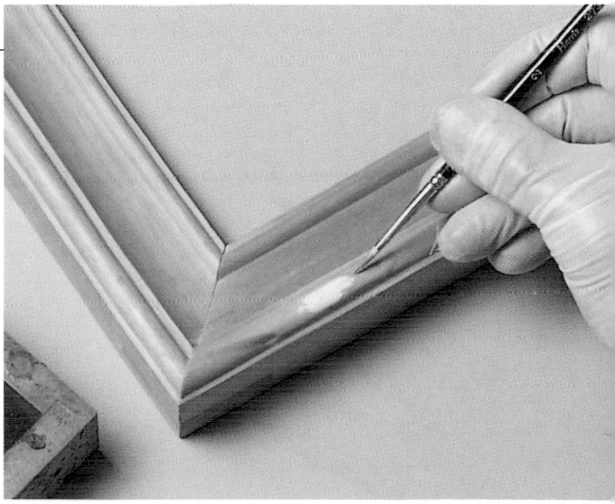

SEE ALSO
Health and safety, page 12
Sanding and scraping, page 30

REMOVING STAINS

PREPARATION

Blue and iron stains are faults within the wood that occur during the kiln drying done by the timber merchant or sawmill. Blue stain is caused by a mold that grows on timber and leaves blue marks that look like ink stains. Iron stain is caused by particles of iron from nails, screws, saw blades, corrugated-iron roofs, and even shrapnel, which react with tannic acid present in the timber. Oak is renowned for reacting in this way. The stains, which appear as black flecks in the grain, usually show up after sanding.

YOU WILL NEED

Oxalic acid
Protective gloves, goggles, and overalls
Glass, plastic, enamel, or earthenware containers
Wooden spatula
Synthetic bristle paintbrush
Cotton cloth
Abrasive papers and dust mask

Oxalic acid is used to bleach dark stains and can also be used for cleaning off dirt from old timber, especially oak, and for degreasing oily surfaces such as teak.

REMOVING A STAIN WITH OXALIC ACID

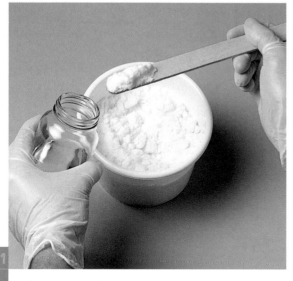

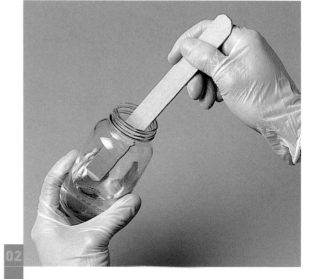

01 Oxalic acid is supplied as a white powder in dry crystal form. Remember that it is poisonous, so always wear protective gloves, goggles, and overalls, and wash your hands after working. Use glass, plastic, enamel, or earthenware containers and a wooden spatula for mixing and storing the crystals. Make a saturated acid solution by adding the crystals to warm water and stirring.

02 Keep adding crystals until no more will dissolve. About a cupful of solution is needed to bleach a tabletop. Always add the crystals to the water, and not the other way round. Leave to stand for about 10 minutes before use.

PRO TIP

When working on a large area, such as a tabletop, use a cleat under the board to prohibit any tendency to bow when dampened.

HEALTH AND SAFETY

- Always wear protective gloves, goggles, and protection over clothing when using oxalic acid crystals and solution.
- Only use bleach in a well-ventilated room or outdoors.
- Follow the manufacturer's instructions carefully and thoroughly.
- If bleach comes into contact with skin, wash with plenty of water immediately.
- Work with a drain or waste pipe within easy reach.
- Wear a dust mask when sanding surfaces after bleaching.
- Store chemicals away from sunlight, in a cool, dark place.
- Always keep bleaches away from children; and never store or use in food containers, in case they are mistakenly eaten or drunk.

03 Apply the acid solution with a synthetic bristle brush, laying it evenly over the stain. Do not splash it, and always wear gloves and goggles. Try not to let droplets fall on the surface where they will mark the piece, and do not saturate the timber with solution, because adhesives may be affected.

04 Leave the acid solution to soak into the timber for about 30 minutes. For very stubborn stains you may need to apply a second coat. Using clean water and a clean, uncontaminated cloth, rinse the treated area.

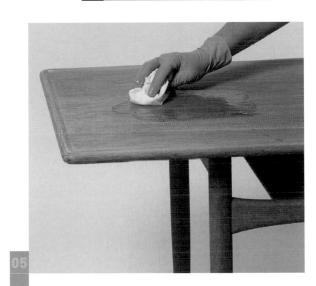

05 It is essential to use lots of clean water to wipe away all traces of the oxalic acid.

06 When you are satisfied that all traces of the acid have been removed, allow the workpiece to dry out thoroughly before sanding down—wearing a dust mask—and refinishing.

SEE ALSO
Health and safety, page 12
Sanding and scraping, page 30

BLEACHING WOOD

Bleaches are used to lighten the color of timber, and are sometimes required if you intend to alter the finished color of a wooden object with a colored wax. There are many different types of bleach, and the household variety can be used on timber, but the best approach is to buy a special wood bleach, sold in a two-part pack, that generates a stronger reaction with the surface.

YOU WILL NEED

Heavy protective gloves, goggles, and overalls
Two-part timber bleach
Two synthetic bristle paintbrushes
Two glass or earthenware containers
Acetic acid (white vinegar)
Soft scrubbing brush
Cotton cloth
Abrasive papers and dust mask

TWO-PART BLEACHES

The bleaches are supplied in two plastic bottles, normally labeled A and B or 1 and 2. The first bottle contains a solution that may darken the timber, and by adding the peroxide solution in the second bottle the bleaching action is activated. It is important to check which bottle is which and they must be kept separate, because mixing them causes a violent reaction and they can even explode. Use equal quantities of each part, without drenching the timber. They will foam on the surface, and bleach the wood by oxidizing.

   For this product a neutralizer is also essential, in order to halt the chemical reaction and ensure that any residue of bleach does not harm further finishes. A 5 percent solution of acetic acid in water is the traditional way to neutralize a two-part bleach, with plenty of water to clean the surface.

01 When working with bleaching agents, wear heavy protective gloves along with goggles and overalls, work in a well-ventilated room or outdoors, and read the manufacturer's instructions before you start. If the article was painted or varnished, it should be stripped, otherwise simply sand clean.

02 You will need two synthetic bristle brushes and two separate glass or earthenware containers to hold the different bleaching agents. Apply the first solution to the wood with a brush, making sure the wood is covered evenly. Leave this solution on the wood for the recommended time (usually approximately 30 minutes).

USEFUL INFORMATION

APPROPRIATE SURFACES
Dark or colored woods

DRYING TIME
Two-part bleaches need several hours to dry.

HINTS AND TIPS

- To stop the bleaching action, wash with clean water.
- Watch out for wide pieces bowing from being damped. Attach a cleat underneath as a precaution.
- If scum forms on the surface, remove it with a scrubbing brush and water.

03 Still wearing all the protective clothing, use the second brush to apply the second solution. The surface will look darker at this stage. Leave for two to three hours or as recommended by the manufacturer. The reaction of the two chemicals lightens the wood, and sometimes this will produce a foam. Leave the piece until the desired effect is achieved.

HEALTH AND SAFETY

- Since bleaches are likely to react with metal (they are used to reverse the effects of iron filings on timber), always use glass or earthenware containers when working with these chemicals.
- Wear heavy protective gloves along with goggles and overalls when using bleach.
- Only use bleach in a well-ventilated room or outdoors.
- Read the manufacturer's instructions carefully and follow the safety advice given.
- Always have plenty of water available, in the form of a bucket and sponge, in case of spillage.
- Work with a drain or waste pipe within easy reach.
- When sanding bleached surfaces, always wear a mask.
- Store chemicals away from sunlight, in a cool, dark place.
- Always keep bleaches away from children; and never store or use in food containers, in case they are mistakenly eaten or drunk.
- If bleach comes into contact with skin, wash with water immediately.

04 At the end of the manufacturer's stated time, the bleach will need to be neutralized. Make a solution of 1 part acetic acid (white vinegar) to 20 parts water. Using a soft scrubbing brush, work the acetic acid solution well into the grain of the wood.

05 Finally, rinse off the vinegar solution using clean water and wipe dry with a clean cloth. Allow the piece to dry thoroughly away from direct heat sources. When dry, the piece is now ready to be sanded—while wearing a dust mask— and receive the finish of your choice.

BLEACHING GUIDE

EASY TO BLEACH	HARD TO BLEACH
Ash	Cherry
Elm	Rosewood
Beech	Satinwood
Sycamore	Padauk
Birch	Ebony
Pear	Wenge
Apple	Black walnut
Hemlock	Jacaranda

TWO APPLICATIONS NECESSARY
Mahogany
Oak
Walnut
Western red cedar
Eucalyptus
Chestnut
Yew
Douglas fir

SEE ALSO
Staining wood, page 62
French polishing, page 84

48

PREPARATION

COLORING WOOD

Wood can be colored with either pigments or dyes. The difference between the two is that dyes are dissolved in a solvent and penetrate into the grain of the wood, whereas pigments are used in suspension and lie on top of the grain. This is why pigments fall to the bottom of a tin, having been mixed with a liquid. They are used for blinding or hiding a defect or knot, or for touching up a polished surface. Dyes are the coloring agents of stains and can be dissolved in spirits (in the case of aniline dyes) or other solvents, such as water or oil.

YOU WILL NEED

Protective gloves
White paper or old white plate, for mixing on
Artists' brush
Selection of pigments and stains
Denatured alcohol and/or French polish (shellac)
Filling knife

DYES AND STAINS

Dyes become part of the timber and are used for matching woods. Their translucence allows the grain to show through. The idea is to use colors to bring out the color inherent in the timber. This might mean adding warmth with a red dye, or even cutting back red hues by using green. The whole piece may need coloring, or just small parts, especially during restoration or when components do not match within a new piece. It is quite common for the legs or rails of a table to have been milled from a different batch of timber from that of the top. As a result, the colors may vary slightly, but this can be rectified using dyes.

Study the wood to determine what colors are needed to match it exactly. The best way to learn is by trial and error, so always test color on a variety of surfaces to see what effect it has. With practice you will understand better the consequences of color, and should be able to judge the match by testing colors on scraps of timber.

Do not try to obtain a perfect match in one go, but gradually blend the color in with a progression of dyes. Try to copy the subtle differences in color and shade of the grain pattern, and apply the color with brushes or mops for small areas, and batting for larger ones. Look for distinctive color or what is known as "natural flash." This refers to the fact that the color is seen from varying angles because of the honeycomb structure of the timber. Wenge has little natural flash, and has a flat, constant color. If possible, color a piece with it standing at the appropriate level. For example, stand a chair on the floor and place a clock at chest height.

Most timbers are shades of brown, ranging from the beige of light oak to the black color of ebony, with countless shades in between. Many woods can be matched using Bismarck brown (which is a reddish color) and spirit black, with green, blue, and yellow for adjustment. Remember that black and red make brown. Look for the colors in the timber.

Right: Opposite colors counteract to bring back the browner side.

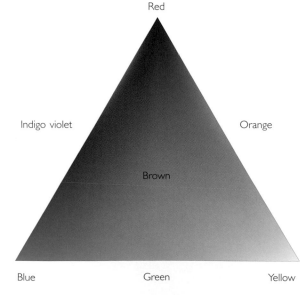

Red

Indigo violet

Orange

Brown

Blue

Green

Yellow

HINTS AND TIPS

- Mix pigments on a piece of paper for quick coloring.
- Mix colors gradually.
- Work in natural light.
- Study color of timber and grain pattern.
- Color the piece while it is standing at the appropriate height, for example stand a chair on the floor.

COMMON PROBLEMS

The most likely mistake is to make the color too dark. Work slowly and gradually. Do not try to achieve a perfect color match in one go.

USEFUL INFORMATION

APPROPRIATE SURFACES

Most woods can be colored, but dyes work better on lighter colored woods.

PREPARATION

Prepare the piece to be colored by cleaning and sanding to remove all traces of grease and dirt.

DRYING TIMES

Refer to manufacturer's instructions.

FINISHING

Stained wood can be finished in many ways, though some sprayed finishes may react with the stains.

PIGMENTS

Pigments have to be mixed together before being applied, in order to produce the correct color. Unlike dyes, they are not translucent, so one layer has little influence upon the next. They have colorful names, but a finisher only really needs about eight different pigments, which can be mixed with denatured alcohol and/or French polish (shellac) to create the desired result. When using pigments in conjunction with polish, add the colored polish to a polishing pad or some batting (see page 50). Pigments are strong and only need to be mixed in very small quantities, using a filling knife to pick up the powder.

Use an artists' brush to apply pigments on defects, keeping a steady hand (see page 43).

MIXING COLORS

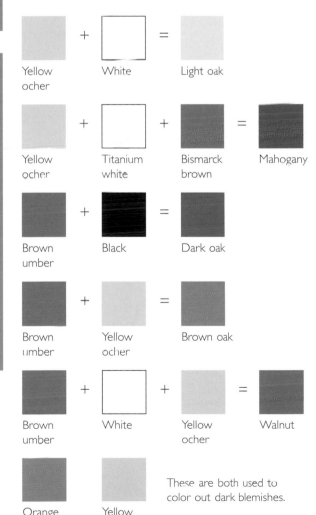

Yellow ocher + White = Light oak

Yellow ocher + Titanium white + Bismarck brown = Mahogany

Brown umber + Black = Dark oak

Brown umber + Yellow ocher = Brown oak

Brown umber + White + Yellow ocher = Walnut

Orange chrome   Yellow chrome

These are both used to color out dark blemishes.

COLOR MATCHING

YOU WILL NEED

Paper
Double-sided adhesive tape
Paper boat (see page 10)
Dye or pigment diluted in
    denatured alcohol or polish
Batting

01

The frame of this mirror unit is slightly lighter in color than the rest of the unit. It needs to be color matched before the piece can be finished. Mix a dye or pigment solution to match the color of the original, and pour it into a paper boat.

02

Mask the mirror glass with paper, stuck down with a few small tabs of double-sided adhesive tape. Use batting to apply the color. Dip the batting into the boat of color, only taking up a little of the liquid. Do not try to use too much color at a time.

03

Squeeze out excess color from the batting onto a piece of paper. Do not do this on the top of the workbench, where the batting is likely to pick up dirt and dust. Squeezing out the batting on paper also spreads the color through the batting, which helps to ensure an even application. Remember that only a shade of color is being applied.

HINTS AND TIPS

• The most common mistake when touching in color is to make the color too dark. Work slowly and gradually. Do not try to achieve a perfect color match in one go.
• Work in natural light in order to achieve the best color match.

04

Wipe the color onto the surface using straight strokes. Follow the grain and keep an even pressure. Do not start applying a second stroke of color until the first has dried. Applying more color to wet color is likely to produce a patchy finish. Build up the color gradually until the required shade is achieved

05

When the color work is done, the frame should match the rest of the piece. The color must be constant. This technique can also be used for matching new veneer that has been let in as a repair.

SEE ALSO
Filling holes, page 40
Removing stains, page 44
Coloring wood, page 48
Repairing veneers, page 58å

RESTORATION

There comes a time when old furniture and other wooden items need a good clean, without resorting to the drastic action of stripping. Indeed, more often than not there is value in retaining the original finish, since it will have developed a mellow patina that cannot be recreated. A patina that has been built up over the years is one of the most attractive features of antique furniture— but, as with paintings, the surface tends to dull with age and the finish may need to be rekindled by thorough cleaning.

YOU WILL NEED

Soap and water
Fine 000 steel wool
Commercial reviver
Protective gloves
Cotton cloth

Cleaning and restoration must be done with great care. It is relatively easy to strip or sand back the wood, but that destroys the finish and detracts from the character of the piece. Always try to conserve, restore, and enhance, rather than remove. Remember that the patina is skin deep and does not penetrate far. The aim should be to give new life to the finish, not to make the piece look new. The beauty of antique furniture lies partly in its used appearance, in the shades and tones the timber has developed over the years.

CLEANING AN OLD FINISH

01

HINTS AND TIPS

- Always test on a hidden area.
- Work slowly and carefully. The aim is to clean the finish, not to remove it.
- Do not sand the surface.
- Try not to make the piece look as if it is newly made.
- If the finish does not react to testing, it is probably a spray finish and will need chemical stripping.

The underframe of this mahogany table needs to be restored. However, dirt has built up over the years, and it must be removed before structural repairs or restoration can be started. The aim is to clean off dirt and grime that has accumulated. Grease and vestiges of food build up on tabletops, while oil from hands has to be removed from the arms of chairs. What is required for cleaning is a formula that will pick up the dirt but leave the patina. Much grime can be removed with soap and water. Gently wash the surface, but do not overwet it, otherwise the timber may move and joints come apart.

02 Use fine 000 steel wool and a commercial reviver to clean off the dirt. Wearing protective gloves, pour the reviver onto a hand-sized ball of steel wool, using enough to dampen it thoroughly.

03 Rub off the dirt and old wax, following the grain. Make sure you work the steel wool into all grooves and corners. Recharge with reviver regularly. Ensure that the reviver cleans the surface of the piece, but that it does not strip off the finish.

04 The reviving fluid produces a sludge, some of which will get caught up in the steel wool. Clean the rest from the surface with a soft clean cloth. Do this frequently because the sludge can discolor the wood. More than one session of reviving may be necessary to remove stubborn grime.

05 Once the piece is dry, apply polish with batting. There is no reason to build up a finish, just wipe over to bring back the sheen.

USEFUL INFORMATION

APPROPRIATE SURFACES
All wood is suitable for cleaning with soap and water. Wax and oiled finishes are suitable for cleaning with reviver, though check the manufacturer's instructions.

FINISHING
Polish, applied with batting.

06 The mahogany table is now clean. Note how the color is stronger and the lines more exact.

RENEWING THE FINISH

After cleaning, fill any small dents with colored or clear beeswax. Some touching in with alcohol stains and polish may also be required. Do not try to obtain a perfect match in one go, but gradually blend the color in with a progression of dyes. Try to copy the subtle differences in color and shade of the grain pattern, and apply the color with brushes or mops for small areas, and cloth for larger ones. Look for distinctive color or what is known as "natural flash." This refers to the fact that the color is seen from varying angles because of the honeycomb structure of the timber. Wenge has little natural flash, and has a flat constant color. Most timbers are shades of brown, ranging from the beige of light oak to the black color of ebony, with countless shades in between. Many woods can be matched using Bismarck brown (which is a reddish color) and black, with green, blue, and yellow for adjustment. Remember that black and red make brown. If possible, color a piece with it standing at the appropriate level. For example, stand a chair on the floor and place a clock at chest height.

Where appropriate a French-polish finish can be rubbed onto the surface with a polishing pad (see page 85), and oiled finishes can be restored using linseed oil.

USING FINISH REVIVER

01 When you have a workpiece that has marks and blemishes that will not polish out, but does not need stripping and refinishing, try finish reviver.

02 Shake the container well before pouring out some of the finish reviver onto a clean cotton cloth, do not pour the liquid directly onto the surface of the workpiece being cleaned.

03 Apply to the workpiece surface with heavy pressure and apply extra liquid cleaner to the areas with waterstains or heat marks.

04 When you are satisfied that the workpiece is as clean as possible and any stains or marks have been removed, finish off by rubbing with a clean cloth or duster.

RESTORING AN INLAID PIECE

Inlay, as on the top of this occasional table, often needs minor repairs. Remove loose pieces of veneer, replacing if necessary, and then color matching (see pages 58–61 and 48–51). Chips on the edge of the piece can be filled with wax (see page 42). The table may have been used as a plant stand, so check for water marks, which can be removed by gentle rubbing with denatured alcohol and linseed oil.

RESTORING A DAVENPORT

Ink stains found on the lid of this Davenport (used as a desk) have been removed with oxalic acid during restoration (see pages 44–45). Loose veneers on the pen tray have been repaired and glued down, and old wax and dirt have been cleaned off the legs.

RESTORING AN ARMCHAIR

The most obvious areas of this armchair that need attention are the screw holes on the back and peg holes at the corners on the rails. These should be filled with wax (see page 42). The arms must be polished to clean off all the dark oil from hands. Check the legs—especially the intricate turning—for marks and dirt, and clean with a finish reviver (see pages 52–53).

TREATING WOODWORM

You are unlikely ever to see a living woodworm (or common furniture beetle), because these creatures are dull brown in color and only 1/8 in. (3 mm) long. The eggs are laid in summer in small cracks in the woodwork or in existing woodworm holes. The grubs hatch after about six weeks, and spend the next year or two eating their way through the wood. Then they pupate, tunnel their way to the surface, and fly away as adults to start the cycle all over again.

YOU WILL NEED

Syringe
Chemical insecticide
Paintbrush

Attacks are usually on the backs of furniture or under framing, and pieces should be checked periodically for any sign of the fine dust that betrays worm activity. If you spot any symptoms of woodworm, take action immediately. Run a vacuum cleaner over the surface to remove the dust from the holes, then treat the holes with woodworm killer. If you detect woodworm in upholstered pieces of furniture, the items will need to be fumigated by a professional company, using a special gas that does not affect the fabric.

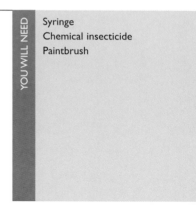

01

When checking wood for the signs of woodworm infestation, you should look for the boring and flight holes (circled top) and/or the burrowing channels of the grub (circled right).

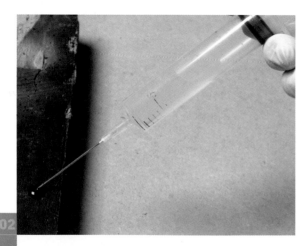

02

Use a syringe to force woodworm killer into the larger holes and enable the medium to reach along the channels.

03

Using a paintbrush, saturate the area with insecticide and allow to dry, following the manufacturer's instructions.

PREPARATION
Use a vacuum cleaner to remove dust from woodworm holes.

DRYING TIMES
Drying times for chemical insecticides vary, so consult the manufacturer's advice.

There are several things you can do to prevent woodworm attacks.

• Treat timber additions, such as moldings or spindles, with a commercial woodworm fluid before you fix them in place. Once the fluid has dried the wood can be stained and polished in the usual way.

• Woodworm grubs cannot penetrate layers of paint, so one way of preventing an attack is to paint a piece of furniture.

• If you do not want to use paint, you can buy special waxes that contain an insecticide. These treatments make an effective deterrent against woodworm, but need to be applied regularly to achieve the maximum benefit.

LIFECYCLE OF WOODWORM

Eggs laid in crevices and open joints in wood

Grub hatches and bores into wood

Grub becomes a pupa near the surface of wood

Beetle bores out of wood, mates, and flies off to lay eggs on new site

The existence of only a few worm holes on the surface of the wood does not indicate that the damage is minimal, as this piece shows. Replace seriously damaged wood with a new section.

SEE ALSO
Sanding and scraping, page 30

PREPARATION

REPAIRING VENEERS

The most common veneer faults are along the edges of drawers or tabletops, often where the cross-banding has been detached. For these repairs it is sometimes best to remove whole strips of veneer and replace them completely, rather than attempt a match. Veneer can also blister, when air has been trapped beneath it or because the glue spread is faulty. This fault can be corrected by bursting the blister.

YOU WILL NEED

Craft knife
Straightedge
Syringe
PVA glue
Veneer to suit
Iron
Paper
Sharp knife
Rasp or file
100 grit garnet abrasive paper
Sanding block

Repairing veneers usually means letting in a piece of matching veneer. The important thing is to choose a good match and cut it correctly, so that the grain runs easily from old to new, with no join showing.

Remember when choosing a veneer patch that grain is as important as color for a good match. Also remember that, if the workpiece has not been stripped back, the patch must start lighter in color than the surrounding veneer, because the finish you apply will darken it.

TYPES OF VENEER

Specialist veneer and marquetry outlets sell a wide selection of cross-bandings and inlays and stock small quantities of veneer for repair work. Keep a store of veneers in a variety of colors because you may have to play around with a few to find a piece that matches, but do try to use a matching timber species—different timbers all change color with time. Shown here is a range of exotic and more common veneers:

1 Bird's-eye maple
2 Plane tree
3 Castello
4 Rosewood, santos
5 European walnut
6 Ash
7 Padauk

INSERTING A PIECE OF VENEER

The most essential tool for repairing veneers is a sharp craft knife. When cutting out faults, try to follow the grain or cut at a tangent to it. Where possible, cut a wavy line because the eye is less likely to be drawn toward such a repair, especially on the more figured veneers. As a result, repairs are generally easiest to disguise on those complex woods.

01 It is possible that the groundwork has also been damaged, and that pieces have come loose. If this has happened, glue any chips back in place and fill any cavities, ensuring that the surface is flat.

02 Trim off the rough edge of damaged veneer using a craft knife and a straight edge. This ensures a neat join. Cut cleanly and firmly, with the straightedge covering the undamaged veneer, so that if there is a slip, the knife will score only the piece to be removed. Use one very light cut to mark the line, then slice through the veneer in a single stroke. Try not to cut into the groundwork.

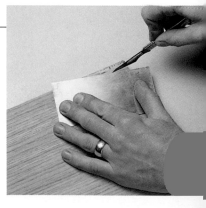

03

Remove all loose pieces of veneer. Using a syringe, apply PVA glue liberally to the area to be repaired. Spread the glue over the area, making sure that there is enough to be squeezed out by the new piece of veneer.

- When using delicate veneers, tape the face with veneer or masking tape before cutting out the new patch. Mark the tape so you can position the patch.
- If you have a number of repairs to make, veneer punches are especially useful. They are designed to cut out the fault from the damaged veneer and a matching patch from the new material. Veneer punches are made in a variety of sizes and have irregular cutters to help disguise the repair. Try to hit a veneer punch with only one hammer blow in order to achieve a clean cut. Sharpen the outside of veneer punches to keep them very sharp.
- Cutting straight across the grain makes a more obvious repair.
- Novice repairers tend not to cut close enough to the shape.
- Too much heat will loosen undamaged veneer.
- Keep glue off the veneered surface whenever possible.
- Check that glue does not react adversely with veneer by testing on an inconspicuous part.

04

Select a piece of veneer for the repair. Try to find a piece that matches the original both in color and grain pattern. Cut it so that the grain follows that of the panel. It is best to cut a slightly larger piece than necessary, and trim it down after the glue has dried. Try to let in the new piece of veneer at an angle of about 30 degrees to the grain.

05

Use a hot iron to speed up the bonding of the glue. Place a piece of paper between the veneer and the iron to avoid marking. Press down hard with the iron for about a minute, then check to see if the glue has dried.

APPROPRIATE SURFACES
Cutting with a knife is best on straight-grained veneers. The cut line is less likely to be seen afterward on figured veneers and on veneers with interlocking grain.

DRYING TIME
Leave PVA glue to dry for 24 hours.

06

Once the glue has dried, trim off any excess veneer. Take off the bulk of the surplus with a sharp knife, and then use a rasp or file, drawing it downward only.

07

Sand down the inserted veneer, using 100 grit garnet paper folded around a sanding block. Keep the block flat and sand along the direction of the grain.

REPAIRING BLISTERS IN VENEER

Blisters in veneer are caused by the veneer lifting, either because air has been trapped beneath it or because the glue spread is faulty. To correct this fault the blister must be burst, which expels the air, then the veneer can be stuck down again with glue.

A similar fault, often found in old furniture, is called "tenting." It tends to occur along joins between veneers or on the edges of panels when water or moisture has worked its way under the veneer. Tenting is dealt with in much the same way as a blister, but make sure the groundwork is dry before attempting to glue the veneer down.

YOU WILL NEED

Craft knife
Pencil
Plywood or pliable wood
Fretsaw or jigsaw
Perspex
Veneer to suit
PVA glue
Syringe
G-clamps
Fine abrasive paper
Sanding block

USEFUL INFORMATION

DRYING TIME
Leave the PVA to dry for 24 hours.

01 Before restoring this Edwardian hall stand it will be necessary to replace the veneer on the umbrella stand area where the veneer has been damaged due to many years of wet umbrellas dripping onto the surrounding area. First find a matching wood veneer and use a craft knife to cut out a piece very slightly larger than the area you are about to replace.

02 Since this repair is on a curved section of the unit, it is necessary to mark out a former on plywood or an offcut of pliable wood. This will act as part of the clamping-up procedure and will help spread the pressure of the clamps.

03 Cut out the former using either a fretsaw or jigsaw, then offer it up to make sure it will fit snug along the repair section.

04 Under the former you could use a strip of clear Perspex against the veneer so that you can see through it to make sure the newly inserted veneer does not move under the clamps. As PVA adhesive will not adhere to the Perspex, any glue escaping from around the newly glued-up area is in no danger to the repair or the unit.

05 When the glue is quite dry, unlock the clamps, remove the Perspex and former, and trim the new veneer to size with fine sandpaper on a block. Be very careful not to pull the veneer's glued surface, only sand with a very gentle action, pushing the sanding block away from you.

STAINING WOOD

Stains consist of dyes dissolved in a medium and are used for coloring timber. They do so by soaking into the grain of the wood, giving it a tint—unlike pigments, used for coloring paint, which lie on top of the surface as solid matter.

The medium, such as water or mineral spirits, carrying the dye determines the characteristics of the stain, such as drying time, compatibility, and spread.

A stain should enhance the grain and improve the appearance of the wood; it needs to be easy to apply, has to be compatible with the finish, and should dry within a reasonable time. It should also maintain its color, without fading. Stains are particularly good at upgrading timber and making unattractive surfaces more interesting.

Although most wood stains are designed to soak into the timber, for exterior work the stain forms a film on the surface, creating an effect similar to paint. Nevertheless, most stains do not offer protection and so need further finishing.

CHOOSING A STAIN

When choosing a stain, select the one that has the most suitable characteristics. The same color can be produced using different types of stain. Color is therefore not the only criterion for selection. Rather, your choice should be determined by a number of important considerations that you need to keep in mind when investigating the various options. For example: How fast do you want the stain to dry? What finish and timber do you want to use the stain with? Will the stained piece be affected by wear and tear? Does the stain have to match an original antique color?

Stains are applied using a paintbrush or cotton, lint-free cloth and excess stain can also be wiped off with the cloth.

A SELECTION OF DIFFERENT STAINS TO SHOW COLOR RANGE
1 Unstained ash. **2** Blueberry. **3** Golden oak. **4** Mid oak. **5** Yew. **6** Rosewood.

HINTS AND TIPS

- Although stains dry lighter, they are darkened by subsequent finishes—so test the effect on an offcut or hidden area first.
- You can always make a surface darker with more stain, but it is impossible to lighten the color without resorting to bleach.
- A dark stain has a stronger effect on a light wood than on a dark one.
- Avoid stain runs by working on the underside of a piece first.
- Always keep a wet edge when applying stain, to avoid patchy color.
- Plan your staining pattern before starting, so you maintain a uniform color.
- Dampen the workpiece very slightly with water to give some idea of the color effects of applying a clear finish before or after staining.
- When trying to match colors, do so gradually. Don't attempt to mix the perfect combination of dyes straight off—rather, use progressive coats of individual dyes.
- Do not use oil stains with spray finishes, because they can cause discoloration and poor adhesion.
- Oil stains penetrate very quickly, so you may find that when you use a brush the first touches remain darker even when dry. It is therefore better to use a cloth for application whenever possible.
- If an alcohol stain is drying too quickly, mix in a little shellac to make application easier.

WATER-BASED STAINS

USEFUL INFORMATION

APPROPRIATE SURFACES
Wood stains can be used on any timber, especially woods with interesting grains that will be enhanced by the stain. Stains are not suitable for MDF.

PREPARATION
Prepare the piece to be stained by cleaning and sanding to remove all traces of grease and dirt.

Stains bite into deep and uneven grain (as occurs in beech), which may show up as dark patches. It is therefore important to prepare rough areas especially carefully.

Faults and end grain often absorb great quantities of stain, which make them look darker. You may therefore need to seal them with a shellac sealer before staining.

DRYING TIMES
- Water-based stains will dry within 24 hours.
- Shellac sanding sealer is usually dry within 30 to 40 minutes.
- Alcohol stains take only 5 minutes to dry.
- Oil stains take about 30–40 minutes to dry.
- Pigment stains dry in about one hour.
- Wax stains should be left overnight before buffing.

Water-based wood stains are water-soluble and therefore less hazardous to the environment. These stains are supplied in various forms, from a dry powder or crystals that are dissolved in water, to polyurethane-based stains. Powdered dyes have been used for hundreds of years, originally being made with vegetable dyes obtained from trees and plants. They are now the cheapest of all stains and can be bought by mail order from finishing specialists (see page 156).

Although the original dyes are no longer available, the man-made alternatives are useful to have around the workshop. The most useful dyes are Van Dyke crystals (brown), mahogany crystals (warm brown), walnut crystals (yellow-brown), and nigrosine (black). You can mix these dyes in order to produce different colors. By changing the ratio of water to powder, you can adjust the depth of color. Always test water-based stains on an offcut before applying them and check the effect of adding a finish. Use plenty of stain, only stopping short of pouring it onto the surface. Water-based stains such as these dry slowly, so you will have time to wipe off the excess with a cloth or absorbent paper.

The top of this Arts and Crafts table is damaged and needs to be repaired, stripped, and restained. The top is removed and repaired, and will be restained using Van Dyke crystals.

YOU WILL NEED

Protective gloves
Wood dye crystals
Glass or earthenware bowl
Wooden stirrer
Cotton cloth
Shellac sanding sealer
Paintbrush
320 grit abrasive paper
Sanding block
Tack rag
Small brush

USING CRYSTALS

Crystals, which dissolve in hot water, were widely used before the advent of water-based acrylic stains. This method of staining produces a brown color, the intensity of which you can control by dilution.

01 Wearing protective gloves, add the crystals to a clean glass or earthenware bowl of boiling water and mix with a wooden stirrer until they have dissolved. The more crystals you add, the deeper the stain color will be, so test as you go on an area that will not show.

02 Wet the area to be stained with clean water applied with a lint-free cloth. This will help the stain to flow evenly.

03 Use the cloth to apply the stain in even strokes, following the grain of the wood.

04 When you have covered the whole area, take a dry, clean cloth and wipe the surplus stain from the surface. Do not rub too hard because you could lift the stain out.

05 When the stain is quite dry (this will depend on conditions, but 24 hours should be ample), coat the piece with shellac sanding sealer in even straight strokes along the grain. Work quickly, keeping a wet edge, otherwise you can puddle the sealer and it will dry unevenly.

06 When the sealer is totally dry, usually within 30 to 40 minutes, lightly sand the entire area with 320 grit abrasive paper.

07 Use a tack rag to remove any dust, remembering to turn the cloth from time to time to offer a clean surface to the wood.

08 Retouch any patches or areas that were not stained with a small brush and the original stain.

ACRYLIC WOOD STAIN

With water-based acrylic stains it is possible to achieve a beautiful consistent finish in a short time. Acrylic wood stains are available in a range of attractive colors and can be mixed to produce subtle hues. Nonflammable, odorless, water-based wood stains can be used on all types of wood. They dry quickly and have no harsh solvents or toxic vapors. Acrylic wood stains don't penetrate the wood, but simply coat the surface. You won't require more than two coats, otherwise the effect can be patchy.

YOU WILL NEED

Acrylic wood stain
Cotton cloth
Protective gloves
Glass bowl
Small brush

01 Using a soft cloth and clean water, dampen the surface of the wood. This will ensure an even coating of the wood stain.

02 Because acrylic wood stains do not give off toxic fumes, they are ideal for small indoor projects. Wearing gloves, decant the stain into a glass bowl and soak a clean cloth in the stain. Apply the stain liberally to the wood, wiping the surface quickly, using broad, sweeping strokes.

03 Apply the wood stain to each surface in turn, and where possible, apply the stain to a flat, horizontal surface to ensure even coverage and avoid runs.

04 Using a clean, slightly damp cloth, wipe over the wet stained surface to spread the color and ensure an even distribution.

05 Using a small, soft paintbrush, touch up any little areas that the wood stain has missed.

SEE ALSO
French polishing, page 84
Spray guns, page 134

ALCOHOL STAINS

These stains are aniline dyes dissolved in denatured alcohol. Professional woodworkers like using them because of the wide range of colors available.

The stains can be applied by brush, cloth, or spray gun (see pages 134–139) and are also used for dipping work. Because of the alcohol base, they can be mixed with shellac for color matching and touching up during the polishing process. However, if coats of shellac are applied later, they are likely to lift the stain and affect the color.

Alcohol stains dry very quickly, which makes them difficult to apply successfully and can result in a patchy finish unless they are applied with a spraygun.

PIGMENT STAINS

This range of finishes is made from finely ground pigments, suspended in a medium. Pigment stains give a semi-opaque color to timber. They are useful for improving low-grade wood, producing greater tone, and making the piece more attractive.

These stains are available ready-mixed in a range of colors and are applied generously with a brush or cloth. Be sure to remove surplus stain, otherwise the color may look patchy, and opaque.

NON GRAIN-RAISING STAINS (NGR)

These are modern stains formulated from soluble dyes mixed in solvents. This is probably the best kind of stain because it fulfils all the wood finisher's requirements of a stain: fast-drying, good penetration, light-fast, and available in a wide range of colors, from dark to very bright. To apply, spray or use a rag or brush.

OIL STAINS

These stains are supplied ready-mixed, usually in cans, the dyes being dissolved in mineral spirits, naphtha, or a similar hydrocarbon solvent. They are classified by wood color, with names such as "dark mahogany" or "light oak." These stains can be used on any timber, and the names are no more than general guides. Oil stains are most commonly used on joinery and are the stains most widely stocked by hardware stores.

These stains are convenient to use and penetrate deeply into the timber. They are useful for working outdoors, since water-based stains take a long time to dry and alcohol stains dry too quickly to allow large areas to be stained.

CHEMICAL STAINS

Chemical stains have been used for hundreds of years and can produce many different effects. Most of them are colorless, and they do not stain the wood but change its color by reacting with chemicals present in the timber. The best-known of these chemicals is probably tannic acid, which occurs in oak. These chemicals are difficult to get hold of in hardware stores, and can be dangerous to use, but they are available direct from suppliers by mail order. The main chemicals used for staining are: ammonia (as a 10 percent solution in water to darken timber), bichromate of potash, sulfate of iron (green copperas), and permanganate of potash.

WAX STAINS

Wax stains are supplied in soft wax form, ready-made in various colors, and are used directly on the timber or over existing stain. Wax stains cannot be used under finishes such as polyurethane or two-part cold-cure lacquers. They are useful for burnishing moldings, carvings, and turned wood.

Apply wax stains with a cloth, like a wax polish, rubbing the wax into the timber.

Left: Teak garden chairs stained silver gray.

YOU WILL NEED

Artists' brush
White or transparent polish
(shellac)
Cotton cloth
Water-based or oil stain

SEALING INLAY BEFORE STAINING

The contrast in color between different inlays may be lost when a piece is stained. To prevent this, apply white or transparent polish (shellac) to seal an inlay before staining.

01 On this rosewood panel with boxwood stringing, the outer inlay is to be sealed, but the thinner, inner one is not. Pick out the inlay carefully so that no part of it is missed, using an artists' brush dipped in white or transparent polish, and be sure to keep to the line. Leave to dry for 15 minutes.

02 Once the sealer is dry, use a cloth to apply the stain over the whole panel. Use a water-based or oil stain, but not an alcohol stain since denatured alcohol would dissolve the polish and ruin the seal. Rub in the stain evenly, applying it wet in circular motions and then straightening up along the grain. Leave to dry.

03 After the stain has dried, the outer, sealed inlay has retained its natural pale yellow color. However, the inner string has absorbed the stain, and has turned a light brown.

FILLING GRAIN

Some timbers, such as oak, have an open grain structure that makes finishes such as French polishing hard to achieve. With these timbers, the open pores need to be filled with a fine powder applied as a paste or liquid. This choking of the grain also makes polishing quicker, because the grain does not have to be filled with polish—which is the alternative time-consuming solution.

Originally, grain fillers were made from plaster of Paris mixed with water and a pigment, but these plaster fillers tended to turn white and show up in the grain. Modern grain fillers are therefore made from a mixture of filling powder, binder, pigment, and solvent. There are many variations on this theme, each recommended for specific tasks, the distinguishing feature being the type of binder used.

Oil-bound fillers are often called patent fillers. They are not recommended for use with nitrocellulose finishes (see page 140), but can be applied before a polyurethane varnish or shellac polish (see pages 82–83 and 84–89). They are easy to use and are supplied ready-mixed. These fillers are sold by weight and in a variety of colors. A selection of mahogany, walnut, and light oak is sufficient to start with. Oil wood stains (see page 66) can be mixed with white fillers, but generally grain fillers are difficult to color because they require pigments that have to be ground into the binder.

USEFUL INFORMATION

APPROPRIATE SURFACES
Grain fillers are popular for open-grained timbers, such as oak and ash. They can also be used on close-grained timbers such as mahogany and walnut.

PREPARATION
Make sure the surface is smooth and dust free.
Wood should be filled after staining.

FINISHING
Seal with a thin coat of shellac sanding sealer.

DRYING TIMES
- Do not leave an oil-bound filler paste to dry for more than 20 minutes.
- Shellac sanding sealer is dry within 20 to 30 minutes.
- Plaster of Paris filler will be dry in about 15 minutes.

HINTS AND TIPS
- Oil-bound fillers can turn white if not allowed to dry thoroughly. They give a patchy finish if not wiped off thoroughly.
- Clarity of finish can be lost with the use of fillers.

OAK GRAIN
Straight-cut American oak (below)
Quarter-sawn English oak (below right)

OIL-BOUND FILLERS

On many open-grained timbers, such as mahogany or oak, it is advisable to fill the grain before applying a finish. This will smooth the surface of the wood, making it easier to reach a high shine finish. Filling the cavities also means that you will use less finish, be it polish or varnish. You can purchase ready-made grain fillers in many colors. If you are using a proprietary brand it will usually need to be thinned with mineral spirits.

YOU WILL NEED

Protective gloves
Oil-bound filler
Mineral spirits
Burlap or coarse cotton cloth
320 grit abrasive paper
Sanding block
Tack rag

01 Wearing protective gloves, follow the manufacturer's instructions to thin the thick paste down to the consistency of toothpaste. Using burlap or a coarse cotton cloth, take a generous amount of paste and wipe it onto the timber surface with a firm circular motion.

02 Leave the paste to dry for about 20 minutes, then take a clean lint-free cloth dabbed in mineral spirits and wipe it gently across the surface, taking care not lift too much filler. Do not leave the filler for more than 20 minutes, otherwise it will harden too much and, in trying to remove the surplus, you will rub it out of the grain.

03 Smooth the surface with 320 grit abrasive paper. Pay particular attention to the end grain. If the piece you are working on has a molding on the end grain it is advisable to use a small sanding block that will take the shape of the mold. This will keep the shape and ensure against oversanding. Remove any dust with a tack rag.

FILLING GRAIN USING SANDING SEALER

Applied over bare wood, sanding sealer is a clear primer that helps fill small cavities present in hard woods, such as oak, ash, and mahogany, and it helps you achieve a smooth, level surface.

YOU WILL NEED

Protective gloves
Abrasive papers
Tack rag
Shellac sanding sealer
Soft paintbrush

01 Wearing protective gloves, rub the item down through the grades, finishing with 320 grit abrasive paper. Pay particular attention to the cavities and corners.

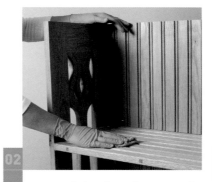

02 Mop up all dust from the item with a tack rag. Where possible, work in a clean, dust-free atmosphere.

03 Apply shellac sanding sealer with a soft brush, working with the grain. Be aware of runs and keep a wet edge at all times.

04 When the sealer is quite dry (about 20 to 30 minutes), rub down very lightly with 360 grit paper. This will ensure that the surface is even and free from runs.

05 Wipe over the entire item again with a tack rag to make sure that the piece is smooth and ready for finishing.

YOU WILL NEED

Protective gloves
Plaster of Paris
Pigments
Wooden spatula
Paper
Burlap
Shallow container

PLASTER OF PARIS FILLER

Although it is a traditional filler, plaster of Paris has a tendency to go white with age. It remains a useful means of flattening rough surfaces (such as chipboard) before applying special paint effects that hide the grain. Plaster of Paris can cause problems if used under acid-catalyst finishes (see page 140).

01 Plaster of Paris is a traditional grain filler that can be mixed with pigments. Wearing protective gloves, mix the pigments and plaster of Paris on a piece of paper.

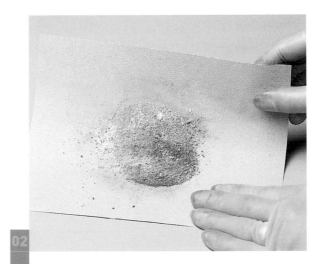

02 The color of the mixed plaster and pigments is roughly the same as it will be once dry in the pores of the wood.

03 Dip a clean piece of burlap into a shallow container of water and then mix with the plaster to create a creamy mixture that is ready to apply.

04 Apply with circular motions, and then along the grain. The filler will dry in about 15 minutes.

CHAPTER 2

BASIC FINISHES

Most woodworkers are introduced to finishing by varnishing their projects. Varnish can be the perfect finish for specific tasks, but there are times when French polishing, oiling, and waxing are more suitable—and they are surprisingly easy to accomplish.

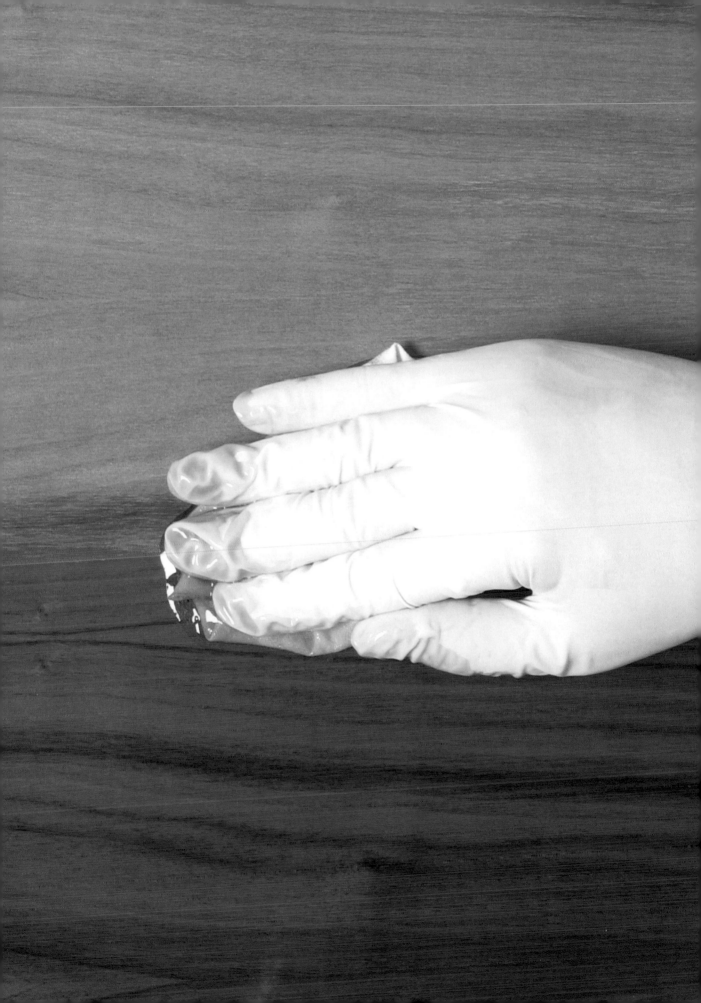

TOOLS AND EQUIPMENT

Oils, waxes, and varnishes do not obscure the natural wood surface, instead they enhance the beauty of the grain, while of course protecting the surface. These effects can include color, luster, or superior shine, all without disguising the inherent aesthetic qualities of the wood.

Standard paintbrushes
These can be used to apply stains, varnishes, undercoats, and glazes. They are made from hog or horse hair.

Pumice powder
Use pumice powder for dulling and as a fine abrasive between applications of French polish. Rub the powder in with a dulling brush (left) or a clean cloth.

Glass jars
Keep a selection of clean glass jars in the workshop, as they are useful for decanting finishes into. This keeps your main supply uncontaminated by air and dust.

Paint kettle
Although metal is not suitable for use with all finishes, a paint kettle allows you to use a small amount of paint at one time, keeping the rest clean.

Small paintbrushes
You will need a selection of small artists' brushes for mixing pigments, matching colors, and working on small areas.

Wax sticks

Manufacturers of wax finishes also make sticks for small repairs. These are colored and designed for use either on surfaces to be waxed or on pieces already polished.

Antique wax polish

Antique wax polish is made by adding a dark stain or pigment to the wax polish. This has a darkening effect on the wood surface, accentuating the grain and building up in the corners of moldings, and is used to impart an antique effect to new and older furniture.

Beeswax

Beeswax is sold commercially, refined and ready for use, as a cake or block. It is also the basis for many manufactured wax finishes. It is usually considered too soft to use by itself, and is often found combined with carnauba to make a more resilient finish.

Wax polish

Wax polish is usually made by blending carnauba wax with beeswax for a yellow polish, or with paraffin wax for a white polish.

Tack rag

Tack rags are sticky open-weave cloths, ideal for cleaning surfaces prior to painting or varnishing.

Carnauba wax

Carnauba, from the Brazilian wax palm, is the hardest of all waxes: its melting point of 365°F (180°C) is much higher than that of beeswax. It is usually blended with a softer wax for ease of application.

Cotton rags

Clean cotton rags are useful for lifting off glazes, creating effects, and cleaning brushes and equipment.

OIL FINISHES

Oiling is one of the oldest treatments for preserving and finishing wood. Originally, linseed oil was used, which is derived from flax and dries by oxidation. Today, oil finishes are becoming increasingly popular because they can be restored and maintained easily—and, unlike varnishes and sprayed finishes, do not conceal the timber's tactile qualities.

YOU WILL NEED

Medium-grit abrasive paper
Cabinet scraper (optional)
Cotton cloth
Mineral spirits (optional)
Oil
Fine silicon-carbide abrasive paper
Tack rag
Fine 0000 steel wool
Protective gloves

Oil finishes do not have the resistance of more modern finishes, and oiled surfaces are likely to become marked, but they can be used on most timbers to bring out the natural qualities of the wood. Teaks, rosewood, afrormosia, and oak are often treated with an oil finish.

Below: Many items of garden furniture—particularly horizontal surfaces—lose their natural luster and color over the winter months. Replenishing wooden furniture with oils will return it to its former beauty and prevent the wood from splitting and warping. Exterior furniture should be oiled regularly to maintain its good condition.

LINSEED OIL

A linseed-oil finish is simple to produce. However, it takes time to dry and new wood will need a number of coats, especially if it is porous. During the complex process of oxidation raw linseed oil actually gains weight as it dries, but it does not dry as quickly as the boiled variety. Boiled linseed oil is partially oxidized and takes a day to dry—compared with three days for pure linseed oil, which is more resistant to external conditions. However, neither linseed oil nor boiled linseed oil are suitable for oiling exterior woodwork.

Warming linseed oil lowers its viscosity and aids penetration. However, it combusts easily, so the safest way to warm it is to pour the oil into a container and stand it in a pot of very hot water.

TEAK, DANISH, AND TUNG OILS

Teak and Danish oils dry faster than linseed oil, and provide a more resistant film on the surface. Teak oil produces a slight sheen; Danish oil leaves a more natural, low-luster finish. These oils are better for new pieces, while linseed oil should be used on older ones. Some of these oils are tinted for color. They all include driers, and sometimes tung oil to enhance their protective nature. You can also buy pure tung oil, which comes from the seeds of the Chinese tung tree and is used in a similar manner to Danish or teak oils.

OIL VARNISH

An even stronger oiled finish can be achieved by mixing linseed oil with an oil-based varnish (see pages 82–83). This produces a thicker coating than oil on its own and also burnishes better.

Apply with a cloth or paintbrush, then leave to dry. For a gloss finish, burnish with a soft cloth once the surface is dry; for a semi-gloss or matte sheen, rub with fine steel wool and wax (see pages 78–79).

APPLYING AN OIL

HEALTH AND SAFETY

- Never leave an oily rag rolled up. As the oil oxidizes, it generates heat and can combust spontaneously. Allow oily rags to dry outdoors, unrolled, whether you need to keep them for further use or you intend to throw them away.
- Nontoxic or edible oils, such as olive oil, must be used for salad bowls and other items that come into contact with food.
- Apply oils in a well-ventilated area away from naked flames.

HINTS AND TIPS

- To thin linseed oil so that it is easier to apply, pour the oil into a container and stand it in a pot of very hot water.
- Enough oil has been applied when patches appear.
- Oil will darken the surface of the wood.

USEFUL INFORMATION

APPROPRIATE SURFACES
Any wood can be oiled. Teaks, rosewood, afrormosia and oak are often treated with an oil finish.

PREPARATION
Make sure the surface is smooth and dust free. If you want to stain the wood, do so before oiling, using a water-based stain because oil stains react with the finish, resulting in patchy coloring.

FINISHING
When finishing thin pieces, there is a chance that they will warp as the oil dries.

DRYING TIMES

- Raw linseed oil takes 3 days to dry.
- Boiled linseed oil takes 24 hours to dry.
- Teak and Danish oils take 12 hours to dry.
- Leave polyurethane oil overnight to dry.

01 Prepare the surface with a medium-grade abrasive paper, sanding in the direction of the grain. For large flat areas, you may find a cabinet scraper is easier and faster to use.

02 Clean off the sanded areas with a soft cloth soaked in water. Naturally oily woods such as teak and iroko may need to be cleaned off further using mineral spirits.

03 Apply the oil to the furniture with a clean, lint-free cloth folded into a pad. Charge the cloth with enough oil to apply a wet, even coat to the surface. Work in a well-ventilated area and away from naked flames.

04 Apply the oil to the wood in long smooth strokes in the direction of the grain to cover the surfaces. Replenish the oil on the cloth as required. It is important to check that the grain is completely wetted, otherwise the finish will turn out patchy. Dispose of used oily cloths carefully because they can heat up and self-combust.

05 You'll need to apply two or three coats of oil, depending on the weather in your region. Allow each coat of oil to dry off before applying the next. Check whether the oil has dried by wiping a hand across the surface and looking for oil marks. Before applying further coats, sand down the surfaces using a fine silicon-carbide paper, rubbing in the direction of the grain and remove the dust with a tack rag.

06 To bring the finished wood to a final sheen, rub in the direction of the grain using a small ball of 0000 steel wool. It's a good idea to wear gloves for this because the steel wool can irritate the skin. Rub in the direction of the grain, keeping an even pressure and stroke over the whole piece to produce a semi-gloss finish. Burnish the surface with a clean soft cloth to remove any dust that might have been left after rubbing with steel wool.

WAX FINISHES

Waxing is a traditional way of protecting and enhancing timber. Wax finishes have been found on Jacobean furniture, beeswax was used by the ancient Egyptians, and to this day wax remains the most popular finish for oak. Indeed, only the introduction of French polishing diminished the popularity and general use of wax. Waxing produces a natural finish; like an oiled surface, it is never complete and repeated polishing continues to improve the finish, deepening its patina over the years.

Beeswax and carnauba wax are the most consistent ingredients of furniture wax. The two are often mixed together with turpentine, by warming, to produce hard but compliant waxes. Carnauba adds strength and is often an ingredient of floor polishes.

APPLYING WAXES

Today, there are many mixed waxes available in cream, paste, or stick form. Some are colored, with the dark antique variety especially good for working old oak. Waxes work well on a stained surface, but should not be used over oil wood stains (see page 66). It is also possible to mix in pigments to achieve special effects. Tinted wax polishes can be used on dark or light woods. The dark waxes are particularly useful for restoration work and for creating antique effects.

YOU WILL NEED

Protective gloves
Shellac sanding sealer
Soft paintbrush
320 grit abrasive paper
Sanding block
Tack rag
Furniture wax
Fine 0000 steel wool
Cotton cloth

Colored furniture waxes are available in many different wood shades.

USEFUL INFORMATION

APPROPRIATE SURFACES
Oak (especially Jacobean oak furniture) is particularly suitable for a wax finish.
   Finishing with polish and carnauba wax works well for turned wood.
   Wax on shellac sanding sealer is appropriate for contemporary pieces made from almost any timber.

PREPARATION
As with any finish, it is important to prepare the workpiece carefully. Make sure any defects in the surface have been dealt with, filling holes and cracks and sanding the surface flat.

DRYING TIMES
• Shellac sanding sealer is usually dry within 20 to 30 minutes.
• Buff beeswax after about 15 minutes.
• Buff carnauba wax immediately.
• Leave the buffed wax for at least 12 hours between coats.

HINTS AND TIPS
• Waxing a surface that has been colored with an oil stain is likely to affect the stain.
• If you try to rub a wax finish too soon, it may break up.

01 While not absolutely necessary, it is a good idea to seal the grain with a coat of shellac sanding sealer before waxing. Wearing protective gloves, apply the sealer with a soft brush.

02 When the shellac coat is dry (about 20 to 30 minutes), lightly sand the area with a 320 grit abrasive paper. Apply light, even pressure, taking care not to break the shellac seal.

03 Use a tack rag to remove all traces of dust.

Apply the wax with a fine 0000 steel wool and rub well into the surface of the wood.

The wax can be applied liberally. Apply with circular movements to make sure coverage is even.

When the wax has dried, but before it goes too hard, buff with a soft clean cloth.

MAKING YOUR OWN FURNITURE WAX

HEALTH AND SAFETY

Always wear safety goggles and a dust mask when working with chemicals or in a dusty environment, and ensure adequate ventilation at all times.

YOU WILL NEED

Protective gloves, goggles, and dust mask
Beeswax
Carnauba wax
Cheese grater
Paper
Saucepan or double water heater
Turpentine
Spatula
Shallow container

Wearing the necessary protective clothing, grate beeswax and carnauba wax into flakes onto clean paper, with 10 parts beeswax to 1 part carnauba.

Melt the wax in a tin or old saucepan over a gas or electric hob, or use a specialized water heater as here. Do not boil the melted wax because this can cause discoloration. Melting takes about 10 minutes.

Remove the saucepan from the heat, then pour 10 parts turpentine to 1 part melted wax into the pan. Stir as you pour, until the mixture is creamy.

When the mixture has reached the right consistency and all the flakes are dissolved, pour it into a shallow container. Leave to cool for some time to produce an even consistency. The polish is ready for use when it has cooled thoroughly.

VARNISHING

Varnishes are available in a variety of forms, with different properties and a range of applications. Unlike polishes, they sit on the surface of the timber as a coat. Some have good waterproofing qualities, others are fast-drying. They are applied by brush, and are available in matte, semi-gloss, and gloss finishes. The matte and semi-gloss varnishes contain a matting agent to produce an irregular surface that doesn't reflect light with the same directness as gloss. A matte finish shows the nature of the timber better than gloss, on which reflections tend to hide the figure.

HINTS AND TIPS

- Decant varnish into a paint kettle and attach a wire across the top so you can wipe off excess varnish from the brush.
- Before varnishing, make sure there is no dust in the workshop. Sprinkle the floor with water and check that your clothes are free from hairs and dust.
- Use a good-quality brush for varnishing. They can be expensive but they can make the difference between a good job and a bad one. A cheap paintbrush would produce a very poor varnished finish. See what's available at your local hardware store.
- Applying varnish before the previous coat has hardened, or even when it is starting to go tacky, is likely to mark the finish.
- Do not stir thixotropic varnishes—stirring breaks the gel formation.

WATER-BASED ACRYLIC VARNISHES

Water-soluble varnishes are faster drying than their polyurethane equivalents and, because of their water base, are nonflammable and the fumes are less toxic. Woodworkers intent on finishing their work in an environmentally friendly manner are experimenting with these varnishes and they are taking over from two-part polyurethane varnishes.

You can purchase brushes specifically for applying acrylic varnishes, and these are a good investment as long as you wash and dry them carefully after use.

YOU WILL NEED

Acrylic sanding sealer
Soft paintbrushes
240 grit abrasive paper
Sanding block
Tack rag
Acrylic varnish
Acrylic varnish brush (or good quality soft brush)

A GLOSS FINISH
See how the candle reflects deeply in the gloss varnish. However, these reflections can sometimes mask the beauty of the wood.

A SEMI-GLOSS FINISH
The reflection is becoming a blur. The details of the candle are less of a distraction to the view of the grain.

A MATTE FINISH
A matte varnish produces the most natural finish, bringing out the color and pattern of the wood and producing little reflection.

01 After preparing your project, in this case with a blue water-based stain, apply an acrylic sanding sealer with a good quality soft brush. Brush in line with the grain and apply quite liberally.

02 When the sealer is dry, usually after four to six hours, lightly denib with 240 grit abrasive paper.

03 Keep the sanding direction constant. Do not use a sanding machine for this operation, as it will take off too much sealer and may damage the wood surface.

04 Remove all traces of dust with a tack rag. Keep changing the exposed surface of the cloth by folding and refolding.

05 Pour some water-based acrylic varnish into a glass dish and apply quite liberally with a soft brush. As you apply the varnish it may look "milky white." This will dry clear after about 20 to 30 minutes.

06 Sometimes air bubbles can appear in the varnish surface as you are brushing. If this happens, brush a thin coat of clean water onto the still-wet varnish. When this water evaporates the bubbles will disappear. Leave your project in a clean, dust-free environment for at least eight hours to dry thoroughly.

07 The finished result. Note that the varnish has dried clear.

TWO-PART POLYURETHANE VARNISHES

These varnishes need an acid catalyst for hardening, and are stronger than standard polyurethane varnishes. They are particularly useful for floors and bartops. They do, however, give off terrible fumes when first applied, by brush, and may react with stains. To achieve a high gloss apply three or four coats and rub down the last coat before burnishing with cream and a cloth. Two coats are sufficient if the varnish is being rubbed to a semi-gloss or matte finish with fine steel wool and furniture wax.

VARNISH STAINS

These varnishes, which are ready-mixed with stain, are supplied in a variety of colors. Some clarity of grain is lost with this type of varnish, but they are useful for covering less attractive timbers. Make sure they are applied evenly in order to maintain a constant color.

PREPARING A BRUSH

It is important to prepare a brush for varnishing, otherwise it will shed bristles and will not soften up. Work the bristles between your fingers, pulling out any loose hairs. Stand the brush in linseed oil, using a wire jig to keep the bristles off the bottom of the container. After a day or so, play the brush backward and forward on brown paper, then clean the bristles using mineral spirits. Straighten the bristles and wrap with clean white paper, fastening with a band around the metal ferrule. Store the brush on its side.

Paper towels are perfect for wrapping up cleaned brushes, as they will absorb any remaining moisture.

APPROPRIATE SURFACES
Any timber surface can be varnished.

PREPARATION
As with other finishes, make sure any defects in the surface have been dealt with, filling holes and cracks, and sanding the surface flat. Varnish is more forgiving than other finishes in that it is a coat that can be cut back flat—but it will exaggerate any blemishes through the refraction of light. Clean the piece first with mineral spirits to remove wax or grease.

Stain the wood, if required, but note that oil-based varnishes will pull off oil stains. Check the base of the varnish before starting. Make sure any stain is dry before applying varnish, and lightly sand with fine silicon-carbide paper if a water stain has been used.

DRYING TIMES
Check the manufacturer's instructions for the drying time and drying conditions for acrylic sanding sealer, although four to six hours is usual.

Varnish takes about six or seven hours to dry, but leave overnight between each coat.

- Varnishes can cause drowsiness, so always work in a well-ventilated area.
- Wear a mask when sanding varnishes.
- Take great care when using two-part varnishes, keeping special thinners at hand and ensuring there is a constant draft.

POLYURETHANE VARNISHES

Polyurethane has become the symbol for home varnishing, since most varnishes in hardware stores are based on this resin. They are available for outdoor use, or with a thixotropic agent to form a gel, which helps on vertical surfaces. Supplied in matte, semi-gloss, and gloss, they flow well and are applied by brush—though the final coat must be laid on with as little brushing as possible to avoid streaking.

YOU WILL NEED

Protective gloves and dust mask
Polyurethane varnish
Mineral spirits
Glass container
Stirrer
Acrylic paintbrush
320 grit abrasive paper
Tack rag

01 Wearing protective gloves, dilute polyurethane varnish with approximately 10 percent mineral spirits for the first coat. Manufacturers of varnishes do not recommend thinning, but it aids penetration. If you have used an alcohol stain (see page 66), apply the varnish carefully using the minimum of brushstrokes, so that you do not loosen or move the stain.

02 Use a clean acrylic brush to apply the varnish with long smooth strokes following the grain. When the surface is completely dry, sand lightly with 320 grit abrasive paper, wearing a dust mask. Sanding will produce fine white dust, but if the varnish starts to tear up into little balls, it is still too soft and you may need to strip it off and start again. Varnish takes time to harden, and though the surface may seem to have set, the same may not be true underneath. Remove any dust with a tack rag and apply more coats of varnish until you have reached the degree of shine you require. Most pieces will need two or three coats.

FRENCH POLISHING

The simple principle of French polishing is to build up a lustrous finish with thin coats of transparent or colored shellac polish (see page 88). The joy of this finish is that it is worked into the surface, rather than laid on top like a paint, varnish, or sprayed lacquer.

Few tools are needed, and the small stock of materials can be bought either ready-mixed or in a raw state for home mixing. Start by buying proprietary brands, then, as confidence grows, you can try mixing your own polish to suit the needs of particular jobs.

YOU WILL NEED

Iron
Brown paper
Very fine abrasive paper
Sanding block
Tack rag
Shellac polish to suit
Batting or cotton wool
White cotton cloth
Soft mop brush (optional)
Airtight container
Protective gloves
Linseed oil

As a general description the term French polishing is now something of a misnomer, as French polish is only one of the many shellac-based products sold by finishing suppliers. However, "French polisher" remains the time-honored title of the skilled craftsmen who undertake this style of finishing.

APPLYING FRENCH POLISH

The essential components of a polishing kit box (shellac, denatured alcohol, and linseed oil, with a polishing pad for application) have hardly changed over hundreds of years, though the original formula for French polish died with its

Parisian inventors in the eighteenth century. When applying French polish, the aim is to avoid creating marks—so the polishing pad is designed to work the mixture of shellac and denatured alcohol evenly across the surface, lubricated by linseed oil.

SEALING THE SURFACE
Once a sealing coat has been applied and the surface has been lightly sanded (denibbed) and dusted, further applications of polish build up the finish.

01

If the surface of the object to be French polished is damp, for example if it has just been stripped and rinsed, you need to remove all traces of moisture. Use an iron on a low heat over a sheet of brown paper to protect the surface and absorb the moisture.

02 When the wood is completely dry, lightly sand, using very fine grade abrasive paper, following the direction of the grain.

03 After sanding, remove all dust, using a tack rag. Any dust left behind will mar the smooth surface appearance of the French polish.

04 Seal the surface with an initial coat of shellac polish (known as "fading up"), using a pad or a soft mop brush. Apply the shellac along the grain of the wood. When dry, denib the shellac by sanding gently across the grain with very fine abrasive paper.

MAKING A POLISHING PAD

01 The polishing pad is used to apply shellac polish. Start by folding a 6 in. (150 mm) square piece of batting in half. (Cotton wool can be used but the result will not be as good.)

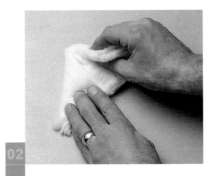

02 Fold over the ends of the batting to make a point. At this stage it will look a little like a pointed hat.

03 Fold the long ends toward the center and tuck them in.

04 Work the batting into a pear shape. It is important that the sole is flat when held between the fingers. The idea is to produce a firm core to the polishing pad.

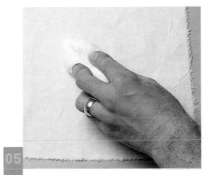

05 Place the batting core diagonally on the corner of a piece of 9 in. (225 mm) square white cotton cloth with the sole of the batting facing downward. The cloth must not be starched or colored.

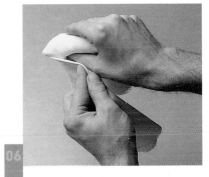

06 Turn the cloth over and hold the core between index finger and thumb to let the folds drop down to the sides. Make a fold to form the point, and turn the ends together under the core.

07 Pull the excess cloth across and start to twist together to tighten.

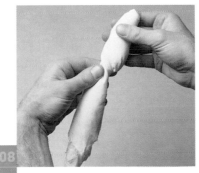

08 Make a final twist, bringing all the loose ends together, and leaving nothing hanging.

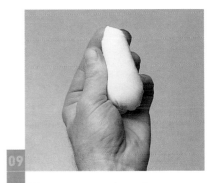

09 When not in use the pad must be stored in an airtight container.

APPROPRIATE SURFACES

French polishing can be used on most timbers. However, it is perhaps most highly regarded on mahogany, because the close grain of the wood is admirably suited to the finish and its attractive figure is enhanced by the "depth" of the polish. Timbers such as walnut, rosewood, sycamore, and stained pine are equally suitable. Oak is less so, and is given a wax finish more often than not.

PREPARATION

To achieve the smoothness of a grand piano (the ultimate aspiration of French polishers, though pianos are now often sprayed), the preparation has to be faultless. If you want a full-grain effect, fill the open pores with grain filler then sand through the grades, making sure the grain has been raised and that you sand it flat.

French polish is particularly sensitive to water and alcohol—as any dining table will testify—so check there is no damp on the surface, which will show up later. If necessary, heat out any dampness with an iron over sheets of brown paper. When staining the piece, remember that the denatured alcohol in the polish is likely to soften alcohol stains and affect the color.

DRYING TIMES

The first coat of polish dries in one hour. Keep bodying up until the surface is too sticky to continue (because it has started to dry)—then leave overnight before embarking on the next bodying up session. It is also best to leave the results of the second bodying up to dry overnight, because it tends to sink.

CHARGING A POLISHING PAD

Use a bottle of polish for charging the pad. For better control of the flow, punch holes or cut a slit in the lid of the bottle.

To load the pad, wearing protective gloves, open up the outer layer of cloth and pour the polish into the core until it is saturated. Squeeze out the excess onto paper or a spare piece of wood.

The polish must soak through the core, but must not then drip through the outer cloth. You need to be able to produce a small trickle by cupping the pad in your hand (with your forefinger running along the point) and gently squeezing the pad.

If you do accidentally overcharge the pad, squeeze out the excess until the steady flow stops, then wipe on a piece of clean scrap to dry off the surface.

Store the pad in an airtight container after use (never store in a metal container). You do not want to throw away a polishing pad, as they take time to break in and a new one is not as easy to use. However, you will have no option but to throw away the pad if it goes hard.

MOTIONS FOR APPLYING POLISH WITH A PAD

Straight strokes must follow the grain

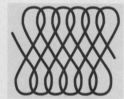

Interlocking figure-of-eight strokes for bodying up

Wide figure-of-eight motions

Interlocking circles to produce an even coat

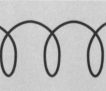

Wide circles for initially spreading the polish

Pressure guide

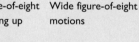

Straight strokes using light pressure

Straight strokes using medium pressure

Straight strokes using heavy pressure

APPLYING THE POLISH

01 Apply the polish with firm but gentle strokes, following the diagrams on page 86.

02 Continue working the surface in figure-of-eights and recharge the pad as soon as it begins to dry out.

03 Continue to work the surface and recharge the pad as required.

04 There are now proprietary brands of "simple French polish" on the market. These can be brushed on with a soft clean brush. The finish on a flat surface won't match the shine and depth of "real" French polish, but the product can be used to great advantage on moldings, carvings, or areas that are not flat.

With several layers of polishing to do, you may feel the pad becoming tacky on the surface. If you do, rub the sole of the pad with a small amount of linseed oil. Then, continue with the polishing as before.

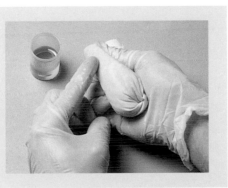

CREATING A HIGH-GLOSS FINISH

For a really high-gloss finish, charge the pad with denatured alcohol only and work over the surface with circular and straight movements. The polishing pad must feel cold to the touch, and not moist. Spiriting off will take off the last of the remaining oil and give the surface a high-gloss finish.

CREATING A SEMI-GLOSS OR MATTE FINISH

A semi-gloss or matte finish is popular because it provides a more natural-looking finish. This can be achieved using pumice powder or wax. There are many grades of pumice. It is essential that a very fine grade is used—300 mesh would be satisfactory.

If dulling with steel wool and wax, do not use too much wax. Once the surface is dry, wipe off the excess with a clean soft cloth to produce a satin finish. The steel wool needs to be fine—either 000 or 0000 grade. However, test the steel wool on a practice piece before dulling, to find out which grade is suitable. Sometimes 0000 steel wool is so fine that it actually glosses the surface.

WHICH POLISH IS WHICH?

The technique is called French polishing, but the polishes used have different names and different applications.

French polish
French polish is brown (it is also known as brown polish), and is used mainly on mahogany.

Button polish
A golden brown color.

Garnet polish
This is dark brown, and is recommended for the renovation of old surfaces.

White polish
White polish is made from shellac that has been bleached and is milky white. It is used for light timbers, such as sycamore and ash.

Transparent polish
Transparent polish is made from shellac that has been bleached and dewaxed.

01 Pour the pumice powder into a shallow tray. Pour carefully, making sure the powder does not spill around the work.

02 Use a dulling brush to apply the powder. Dip the brush into the powder, taking up only a small amount at a time. Do not use too much—it makes no difference to the finish and will only have to be cleared up to avoid contaminating other finishes.

03 Work the pumice powder against the piece by following the grain, making sure that all areas are covered and treated evenly. Pumice powder should be kept clean, and stored in a dry place.

MATCHING COLORS FOR TOUCHING UP

Any discrepancies in the color will show up once the polish has dried. Wooden pins in chair joints may be too light, and there may be shading around joins in veneer. Stand back and take a good look at the piece to get an overview of the finish. Color irregularities will need to be touched up and disguised. Look carefully at the surface to judge which colors are visible, or lacking, in the timber.

Use alcohol stains (see page 66) for matching colors, and mix them in with the polish. Go easy with these stains, since the colors are strong and are only required in a much diluted form to produce a tint. Remember that it is easier to make a surface darker than lighter, so mix colors gradually.

HINTS AND TIPS

- Always keep the pad well charged—but never with too much polish.
- Use linseed oil sparingly—little and often is best.
- Try to maintain an even pressure when using the pad.
- Work in a dust-free environment.
- To clear excess polish from a pad, simply press it down onto a clean surface.
- Keep your fingernails short—they can scratch the surface and collect dirt, which then falls on the piece during polishing.
- Try to keep the workshop at about 65°F (18°C) for polishing. A cold or humid environment can cause "chilling" in the finish, similar to the white rings produced by hot water or alcohol.
- Uneven pressure while bodying up can create ridges.
- Concentrating only on the center of the piece will create a sheen there, but not in the corners and along the edges.

01 The scratch on this piece has removed the color and revealed the raw timber. The damage can be touched up using alcohol stains.

02 Mix the alcohol stains together by adding a small amount of stain to a 50:50 solution of polish and denatured alcohol, using an artists' brush. Compare the color against the workpiece by dabbing it onto a scrap of wood or a piece of card.

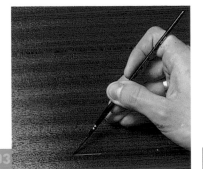

03 Use the tip of the brush only to touch up the scratch, and keep your hand as steady as possible. Build up the repair gradually, with a small amount of color at a time until it matches the surrounding area. Try to imitate the grain pattern as you brush.

04 Do not touch up in one application, but build up gradually. Once the scratch has been repaired it must be polished to match the rest of the surface.

EPOXY RESINS

Epoxy resins refer to a family of molecules or oligomers containing more than one epoxide group. These products are solid or liquid with the consistency of honey and have the ability to react via the epoxy end group to generate three-dimensional networks, providing the final material with rigidity, hardness, and the inability to reflow. The final products generally exhibit excellent electrical properties, good adhesion due to presence of polar groups, low shrinkage, good impact resistance, and moisture resistance.

YOU WILL NEED

Masking tape
Protective gloves
Measuring cups
Two-part epoxy resin
Stirring stick
Paintbrush
Hot-air gun
Fine abrasive paper
Burnishing creme
Cotton cloth

This family of thermosets is used in many applications, such as composites, coatings, adhesives, and encapsulating materials. The chemical chosen to react with these epoxides is referred to as the curing agent (or hardener), and it typically has active hydrogen attached to nitrogen, oxygen, or sulfur. Amine curing agents are the most common and can be primary or secondary, aliphatic or aromatic, or cycloaliphatic. The selection of the curing agent depends on many parameters and will determine, to a large extent, the performance of the final epoxy thermoset. The amines typically have greater than three reactive sites per molecule that facilitate the formation of a three-dimensional polymer network when mixed with the epoxy resin. While the reaction of amines and epoxides occurs at room temperature and below, care must be taken in this selection of curing agent to ensure that a complete reaction takes place. Amines designed for room-temperature application typically employ plasticizers to insure complete reaction. Amines designed for heat-cured reactions use little or no plasticizers and typically give thermosets with higher strength and thermal performance.

The most common epoxy resins are glycidyl ethers of alcohol or phenolics. Liquid epoxy resin is the diglycidyl ether of bisphenol A (DGEBA) and represents more than 75 percent of the resin used in industrial applications.

01 Mask the edges of the wood section, overlapping the surface to be treated. The masking tape should frame the surface to be treated, in order to hold in the resin.

02 Wearing protective gloves, measure out equal parts of resin and hardener.

03 Mix together the two substances by stirring for two minutes.

04 Pour the mixed resin over the surface as evenly as possible.

05 Now use a paintbrush to smooth the resin out over the surface before allowing to settle for two minutes.

06 Using a hot-air gun, apply gentle heat to the surface to remove air bubbles that may have generated through the mixing process.

07 Leave for four to six hours to harden. Ensure that the drying location is dust-free, and with a constant temperature, since problems with the drying conditions will affect the finished result.

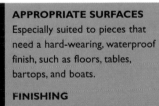

HINTS AND TIPS

APPROPRIATE SURFACES
Especially suited to pieces that need a hard-wearing, waterproof finish, such as floors, tables, bartops, and boats.

FINISHING
Burnish to required luster with burnishing creme.

DRYING TIME
Epoxy resin takes four to six hours to dry.

08 When the surface is completely dry, remove the masking tape. Sand the edges of the wood section using a fine abrasive paper. Use a cotton cloth to apply burnishing creme to the hardened resin surface and burnish to the required luster.

CHAPTER 3

DECORATIVE FINISHES

Decorating timber with special effects is a craft that has developed with the demands of the market. Fashion and ideas from interior designers have influenced the use of these finishes, and craftspeople have evolved their own techniques and designs. As a result, a wide range of processes and effects is available for the finisher to emulate or use as a medium for innovation.

TOOLS AND EQUIPMENT

Brushes are an important part of any finisher's equipment, and most suppliers offer a variety of designs for specialist applications. They are made of different bristles and hairs, both natural and synthetic, and there are many different names given to those brushes. Generally, the higher the price, the better the quality of bristle and brush. In the long run, it is worth purchasing quality brushes. Sable artists' and round brushes are the most expensive, but bring the best results.

Mottler brushes
Mottlers are available in squirrel, hog hair, and even sable. These are graining brushes, used for figuring or drawing the grain, normally after the undergraining is complete.

Graining combs
Combs come in rubber, leather, and steel. A triangular rubber comb with differently graded teeth is a useful first choice.

Stencil brushes
These are specifically designed for stenciling. They are shaped like shaving brushes and are used with a dabbing action.

Gilders' cushion, tip, and knife
When gilding with loose-leaf gold leaf, you will need a gilder's cushion, tip, and knife to convey it to the prepared surface.

Sword liner
A sword brush has long soft hair and an angled face which enable it to travel long distance without having to be replenished. It's often used for veining in marbling. Care must be taken to reshape it after washing.

Flitch brushes
You will need a selection of small-headed flitch brushes for touching up colors and finishes.

Cutting mat and tracing paper
Cutting mats, tracing paper, and craft knives are useful for creating stencils.

Stippling brush
Made from coarse hog-hair bristles and used to produce a decorative stippled effect.

Dragger
Draggers are used for graining.

Graining brush
These are for use in the graining process and are made from hog hair.

Badger-hair softening brushes
Badger-hair softeners are probably the most important members of a specialist collection. They are very expensive indeed, but once you have experienced using one for softening of marbling, you will find the effects hard to equal.

Swan and goose feathers
Feathers can be used in marbling, as an alternative to fine artists' brushes or sword liners. Any clean and relatively sturdy feather will do.

Graining roller or rocker combs
These are available in different widths and grades. They are normally made of rubber and pulled across the wet glaze with a gentle rocking motion to produce a heart grain wood effect.

SEE ALSO
Preparation, pages 24–71
Varnishing, page 80

GRAINING

Graining is thought to date back to ancient Egypt where a shortage of wood stimulated the development of techniques to imitate woodgrain. Similar faux, or imitation, wood finishes later emerged in Europe in response to demands for hard-to-obtain or exotic woods.

HEALTH AND SAFETY

When working with oil-based glazes, do so in a well-ventilated area.

Spread out cloths that have become saturated with glaze and leave to dry before disposing of them. Wet cloths have a low flash point and can combust.

Today, techniques have become highly sophisticated and capable of producing effects that are indistinguishable from the original. Some of these are complex, but you can achieve effective finishes more simply. The techniques shown here have been simplified as much as possible to give an attractive effect with the least amount of effort.

As with most faux finishes, a feeling of depth is achieved by layering the different colors. In most cases the medium is transparent oil-based glaze. The ground color should be a shade lighter than the palest part of the wood being copied, and the graining color, or top coat, should be a shade darker than the darkest part.

Before attempting to reproduce the grain of any timber, take a good look at the natural wood. Compare it with other woods to identify its distinguishing characteristics, and try to memorize its grain pattern and color. It may also help to have a piece of the relevant timber on hand when working to act as a guide.

USEFUL INFORMATION

APPROPRIATE SURFACES
The ideal surface for a grained finish is MDF, which has no obvious grain and needs minimum preparation. However, real wood in poor condition can be overpainted and given a painted grain.

PREPARATION
Make sure the surface is smooth and dust free. Absorbent wood can be sealed with shellac sanding sealer.

FINISHING
It is a good idea to protect your work with a matte or semi-gloss varnish.

DRYING TIMES
Let undercoat dry overnight. Let the glaze dry for 24 to 48 hours before varnishing.

OIL-BASED GLAZES

Glazes have a slower drying time than paint, so allowing the decorative finisher time to manipulate the color to achieve the desired effect. This is particularly useful for graining, marbling, stippling, and rag-rolling finishes. Glazes can be bought ready-mixed with color, or you can make your own.

Transparent oil-based glazes can be tinted with artists' oil paint to achieve a specific shade, particularly useful for woodgraining and marbling techniques. However, because of their high linseed oil content, these glazes have a propensity to yellow with age. Alternatively, a white oil-based paint or undercoat can be added to oil-based glaze, which reduces its transparency and slightly flattens the finish, but also retards the yellowing. Adopting this route, instead of tinting the glaze with artists' oil color then adding white, you can simply add a pretinted eggshell or undercoat to the glaze. Use 30 percent oil-based eggshell to 70 percent glaze, or 20 percent undercoat to 80 percent glaze, then thin by approximately 20 percent mineral spirits to 80 percent tinted glaze. This should result in a glaze with the consistency of whipping cream.

Oil-based glazes should be applied over oil-based base coats, such as undercoat or oil-based eggshell.

GRAINING BY ROLLER

YOU WILL NEED

Undercoat
Paintbrushes
Silicon-carbide abrasive paper
Oil-based glaze
Graining roller
Cloths for cleaning roller

Graining rollers offer a quick method of achieving a wood-like effect with a minimum of effort. There are many different sizes and grades of roller on the market. The term "roller" is slightly misleading; a key part of the action needed to use this device is more like rocking. This movement is made while you pull the roller across the surface. You will need to wipe the roller clean from time to time to prevent it from clogging with glaze.

You can use this technique in conjunction with wood shades of undercoat and glaze, or using colors of your choosing for a range of results.

01 Apply the undercoat and allow to dry before lightly sanding. Brush on the glaze and lay off in the direction that the new grain will run.

02 The open edge of the graining roller must be the leading edge when pulling through the glaze.

03 Hold the roller between fingers and thumb and drag it across the surface, rocking it gently at the same time. The rocking motion should be like turning a key in a lock. When beginning the drag, lean the roller so that the open edge is in contact with the surface. As you perfect the technique, keeping the roller at a constant angle, you can alter the attitude to its direction to achieve an undulating pattern, like watered silk.

CLAIR BOIS

Clair bois, meaning pale wood, is an easy finish to achieve and can be extremely effective.

YOU WILL NEED

White undercoat
Paintbrushes
Silicon-carbide abrasive paper
Raw sienna oil-based glaze
Flogging brush

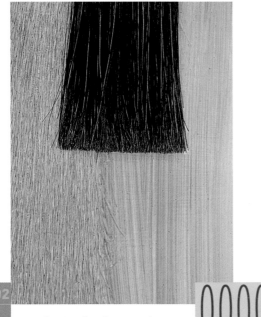

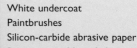

01 Paint on a white undercoat and sand when dry. Brush on the oil–based glaze. To lay off, wipe the brush on the side of the can and use long, even, light strokes to reduce and eliminate brushmarks, working in the direction in which the new grain will run.

02 Use a flogging brush to pat the glaze so that almost the entire length of the bristles is in contact with the surface. Work away from your body, lifting the flogging brush off the work before patting.

03 The finished effect closely simulates a pale wood.

BIRD'S-EYE MAPLE

A bird's-eye maple effect is extremely attractive for small pieces, such as boxes or mirror frames.

YOU WILL NEED

Honey undercoat
Paintbrushes
Silicon-carbide abrasive paper
Raw sienna and raw umber
  oil-based glaze, mixed two parts
  raw sienna to one part raw
  umber
Hog-hair mottler brush
Thin gloves
Badger-hair softening brush

01 Paint on a honey undercoat, allow to dry, and sand lightly. Apply the raw sienna/raw umber glaze mix and lay off, working in the direction in which the grained effect will run.

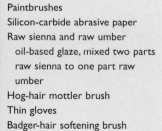

02 Drag a hog-hair mottler across the surface, moving one edge of the brush slightly in front of the other, and then the reverse, in an action like walking.

03 Wearing thin gloves, dampen the tip of your finger and touch the wet glaze to create the bird's-eye marks. These should be scattered over the area in vague groupings. Try to avoid making the prints too contrived or you may get a polka-dot effect.

04 Soften the entire surface using a badger-hair softening brush in all directions. This brush is so soft that it barely supports the weight of its stock. It should be used so delicately that the tips of the bristles barely touch the surface during the stroke, and it will gently blur the glaze into a softer effect.

MAHOGANY

This finely figured wood has been felled indiscriminately and as a result is now virtually impossible to buy. Apart from recycling old items, graining could be your only option if you want the look of this beautiful wood.

  The graining of this wood is more complicated than the two earlier examples because there is more than one application. The undergrain is allowed to dry before first a figuring glaze and then the overgrain are applied on top. The ground color for mahogany should be a brown terra-cotta hue, but an exact match is not necessary.

YOU WILL NEED

Brown terra-cotta undercoat
Paintbrushes
Silicon-carbide abrasive paper
Undergrain glaze: one part raw umber, one part raw sienna, and one part Van Dyke brown
Figuring glaze: one part burnt umber and one part Van Dyke brown
Overgrain glaze: burnt umber
Hog-hair mottler brush
Badger-hair softening brush
Flogging brush
Cotton cloth

01 Apply a brown terra-cotta undercoat and sand lightly when dry. Apply a thin layer of undergrain glaze and lay off in the direction of the new grain.

02 Drag a hog-hair mottler brush through the glaze in the direction of the proposed grain to produce even coloring and a faint drag.

03 Continue with the mottler, this time used at a 90-degree angle to the previous strokes. Maintain this attitude as you etch in the annular rings, starting at the bottom with the smaller ring and building up. In this way the bands get larger as they reach the summit of the figure and reduce as they fall level with the center.

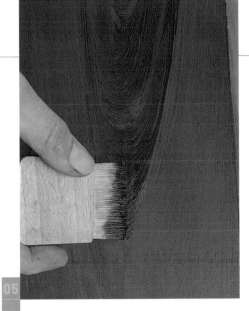

04 Once you have put in the main figure, gently drag in the remainder of the area with the mottler returned to its original attitude. A slight movement of the hand similar to the technique used for bird's-eye maple (see page 99) will feather the edge. Leave to dry.

05 Using the mottler and the figuring glaze, repeat the technique in Step 3, however, the glaze is now being applied instead of being removed.

06 Soften the figuring from the center outward with a badger-hair softening brush and allow to dry.

07 Apply the overgrain glaze, laying it off in the direction of the grain.

08 Pat the glaze with a flogging brush, working from the bottom upward, using a similar technique to that of clair bois (see page 98).

EBONIZING

The rarity and expense of ebony as a natural timber has made ebonizing a popular imitative finish, especially on reproduction Regency furniture and as a substitute for black Chinese lacquer. Traditional ebonizing tends to obliterate the grain to give a uniform finish. An alternative method of ebonizing, that allows the grain of the timber to show through, giving a much better simulation of ebony, is to use a dilute solution of sulfuric acid and a hot–air gun.

YOU WILL NEED

Protective gloves
Sulfuric acid
Measuring cup
Paintbrush
Hot-air gun
Flexible silicon-carbide pad
Tack rag
Cotton cloth
Transparent polish (shellac)
Finishing spirit

01 Wearing protective gloves, mix seven parts water to one part sulfuric acid, adding the acid to the water. Use a paintbrush to apply the dilute mix to the surface.

02 Apply heat to the wet area using a hot-air gun. The heat will turn the timber black.

03 Repeat until the item is completely covered, and allow to dry.

04 Denib the treated surface using a flexible silicon-carbide pad until smooth. Wipe off the dust with a tack rag.

05 Use a cloth to apply several layers of transparent polish until you achieve the required depth of finish. Allow to dry for several hours.

USEFUL INFORMATION

APPROPRIATE SURFACES

To simulate the grain structure of ebony and produce a smooth surface, use close-grained timbers such as beech, sycamore, or mahogany, although interesting effects can be accomplished on open-grained surfaces.

PREPARATION

Ebony is a very dense timber, with very little grain. It is therefore essential that any piece to be ebonized is prepared thoroughly with all the holes and pores filled in and sanded flat. The slightest blemish will be shown up and exaggerated by the finish. Any idea that black masks faults is unfounded, in fact it shows up mistakes more than other colors.

HEALTH AND SAFETY

- Always add the acid to the water.
- Take care not to get too close to the surface with the hot-air gun.

06 Spirit off using a clean cloth and a finishing spirit to achieve a glossy finish.

STENCILING

The beauty of stenciling is that it allows anyone to enhance the simplest of finishes with elaborate and attractive decoration.

In America, settlers decorated their homes with stenciling, and the effect became a measure of status. The patterns, which were usually carried out on a pale background, were taken from pictures or drawn and cut freehand. Today, patterns for stenciling can be bought ready-made from craft stores, and you can use a photocopier to enlarge or reduce images for tracing.

USEFUL INFORMATION

APPROPRIATE SURFACES
Furniture, doors, drawers, walls, and floors. Also, boxes, toy chests, and other decorative items.

PREPARATION
Make sure the surface is smooth and dust free. Absorbent wood can be sealed with shellac sanding sealer. A matte latex paint can also be applied. Stencils are generally applied on a light or pastel background, but there is no reason why the pattern should not be picked out in bright colors against a darker background.

CHOOSING STENCIL DESIGNS

The ability to produce repetitive designs is one of stenciling's most obvious features, and stenciled borders are particularly popular. Equally, single identical motifs on a series of doors or drawers can look most effective.

Floral and ribbon designs are widely available, and can easily be copied from pictures or even wallpaper. Use a photocopier to enlarge or reduce a design to suit the requirements of a particular piece.

Try to use a stencil that is appropriate for the piece. Animals always look good on toy boxes and cupboard doors. Children's books are a good source for designs, but animal stencils are sold by most craft stores and some stationers and toy stores. Fruit and other everyday objects are equally suitable and especially rewarding for children, who can pick out the different images. A sequence of shapes can be made to look more interesting if no one image is painted in a particular color more than once.

As far as possible, blend the shape of the design to the shape of the piece being decorated. The idea is to enhance the piece, not to impose an unsuitable image that confuses the eye.

Below, from left to right: acrylic paint, 25mm brush, stencils, acrylic paints, craft knife for cutting out stencils, two different size stencil paint brushes, pencil for marking out, roller for applying paint, and sponge for paint effect.

MAKING A STENCIL

YOU WILL NEED

Tracing paper
Soft pencil
Acetate
Marker pen for acetate
Straightedge
Craft knife or scalpel
Glass sheet with masked edges
Masking tape
Artists' acrylic paints or specialist
  stencil paints
Stencil brushes
Paper
Cotton cloth

Almost any material can be used for the stencil, but clear acetate is best. It allows the paint or finish to be wiped off easily. Acetate can be difficult to cut, because it has a tendency to split, but, being clear, it can be used for direct tracing.

Start with simple designs, without cutting out large areas of the stencil. If too much rigidity is lost, you will find that it is difficult to manage the stencil while applying the finish. As the patterns become more complex, bridges will be needed to keep the stencil stiff. Cut these bridges as thin as possible, then the unpainted areas can be touched up after stenciling, if required.

Multicolored patterns are produced by using a number of stencils, and it is important to make sure all the stencils are compatible. Do so by punching holes in the corners of each one, then line the holes up with marks on the original drawing or tracing. The holes can also be used for reference when applying the finish.

Draw out the motifs for the design on tracing paper, using a soft, dark pencil.

Position the motifs centrally under the acetate sheet. Make sure there is at least a 2 in. (50 mm) border around the pattern, for support. Large motifs may need a wider border. Also, bear in mind that you may want to use the edges as a reference when you are applying the finish. Trace the motifs onto the acetate with a marker pen.

Using the point of a fine, sharp craft knife or scalpel, cut carefully around the outlines. It is best to use a sheet of glass as a cutting board (pad the edges with masking tape). This avoids the possibility of the blade being deflected by old cut marks, which can happen on cutting boards made from other materials.

FINISHING

It is a good idea to protect your work with varnish. One effect worth trying is a single coat of matte varnish over two coats of gloss. This softens the glossiness a little.

COMMON PROBLEMS

The finish will creep under the stencil if it is not pressed hard enough. This also happens if the paint is too thin, or too much paint is applied.

Do not split a motif in half at the end of a stencil. The line will always show.

DRYING TIMES

- Allow at least four hours for the latex paint base coat to dry before stenciling.
- Leave the stencil finish for 30 seconds before removing the stencil.
- Allow to dry overnight before varnishing.

USING COLOR FOR STENCILING

When stenciling, you are attempting to produce an overall effect—so make sure the colors used are compatible. Floral stencils often look best in pastel shades, while silhouettes and geometric patterns generally benefit from strong, contrasting colors.

Try also to keep the stenciling sympathetic to the piece. Older items may need faded colors to suit their age, while modern furniture with hard lines can take stronger colors and bold decoration. When applying a stencil pattern to wood, bear in mind the color and figure of the grain.

If applied carefully, stains can be used instead of paint for stenciling. They will let the grain show through but tend to creep and spread rapidly, though pigment stains (see page 66) can solve the problem.

APPLYING THE FINISH

The position of the stencil pattern on the object is important, so try it out first, marking off reference lines along the edges with chalk, which can be wiped off later.

Water-based paints, such as artists' acrylics or specialist stencil paints, dry quickly, which makes them the perfect choice when coloring the stencil shapes. Mix the color to suit, making sure you mix sufficient for the job because it will be difficult to reproduce the exact color later. Try not to make the paint too thin, otherwise it will run under the stencil. It can be a good idea to decant the paint to shallow dishes to help keep the amount of paint on the brush to a minimum, and so reduce the chance of creep.

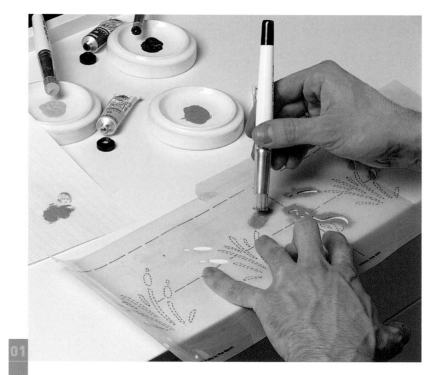

01

Use masking tape to attach the stencil to the workpiece, making sure it fits as snugly against the surface as possible. Any gaps will allow the paint to creep, producing a poorly defined and untidy finish. Dip a stencil brush into the paint and then dab it on some spare paper to ensure the brush is not too heavily loaded. Apply the color by dabbing with the stencil brush in a vertical position.

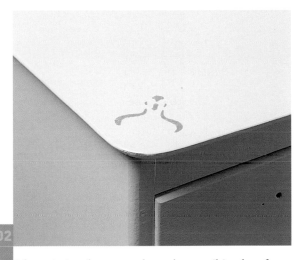

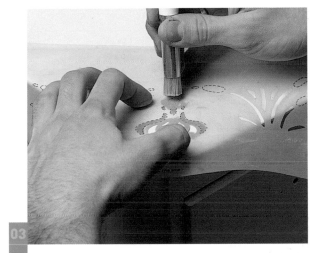

02 After painting the pattern, leave the stencil in place for at least 30 seconds, then remove vertically in one action. This may need some practice. Wipe off any excess paint from the stencil using a damp cloth, and dry with a dry cloth. When creating a repetitive pattern, make sure the stencil does not disturb the previous motif as you move on. Sometimes the stencil will have to overlap; in which case wait until the paint is dry, and in the meantime work on another area.

03 To apply a second color to the same motif, wait until the first motif has dried, then reposition the stencil and dab with the stencil brush as before.

04 Any combination of colors can be used, but always make sure each application is dry before attempting the next, and keep the stencil clean at all times. Three colors have been used here. Notice how the stalks of the flowers are a dark color and the emphasis is given to the flowers and seed pods, which are brighter.

05 This stenciled object has an informal appeal, and would suit a child's room well.

CRAQUELURE

Craquelure is a two-step varnish that produces hairline cracks in the varnish coat, imitating those seen on antique pieces of furniture. The cracks can then be emphasized using artists' oil paints.

YOU WILL NEED

Paintbrush
Matte latex paint
Silicon-carbide abrasive paper
Varnish brushes
Two-part craquelure varnish
Artists' oil paint
Cotton cloth
Mineral spirits

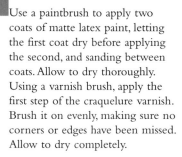

01 Use a paintbrush to apply two coats of matte latex paint, letting the first coat dry before applying the second, and sanding between coats. Allow to dry thoroughly. Using a varnish brush, apply the first step of the craquelure varnish. Brush it on evenly, making sure no corners or edges have been missed. Allow to dry completely.

02 Paint on the second step of the varnish with a new varnish brush, brushing on a medium-thick, even coat. The size of the cracks made by craquelure varnish will be determined by the thickness of the second coat. Brush the varnish on thickly to achieve larger cracks, or apply a thinner coat for smaller cracks. As the varnish dries the cracks will appear. Leave overnight to dry completely.

Small boxes take a craquelure finish well, whereas a dining table is probably too big. On larger items lay the top coat on heavier and wetter than for small pieces, in order to produce a generous "crazy paving" pattern.

APPROPRIATE SURFACES
For this finish the surface is painted solidly, so it is perfect for MDF or a wood that does not have an interesting grain or color. Real wood in poor condition would also be a good candidate for painting.

PREPARATION
Make sure the surface is smooth and dust free. Absorbent wood can be sealed with shellac sanding sealer.

FINISHING
Seal with matte or semi-gloss water-based varnish, or the medium recommended by the craquelure manufacturer.

COMMON PROBLEM
Uneven application produces an uneven pattern.

DRYING TIMES
- Allow at least four hours for the latex paint to dry before applying craquelure.
- Craquelure drying times vary, so follow the manufacturer's recommendations.
- Allow to dry overnight before varnishing.

03 Squeeze artists' oil paint onto a cotton cloth and rub it over the dry craquelure, making sure it gets into all the cracks.

04 Rub back the oil paint with a clean cloth so that the color remains in the cracks only. You will need to switch to a new clean cloth several times. If the oil paint remains steadfast, pour a small amount of mineral spirits onto a clean cloth and rub it lightly over the surface, leaving the paint in the cracks intact. Rub down again with a clean cloth.

SEE ALSO
Preparation, pages 24–71
Varnishing, page 80

DECORATIVE FINISHES

110

CRACKLE-GLAZE

Crackle-glaze imitates the look of paint that has cracked and peeled away from the surface over the years. The crackle-glaze medium is sandwiched between two layers of paint, and causes the top coat of paint to crack. If the crackle-glazing is done neatly and carefully, the texturing can be subtle and refined. The cracks stand out well when contrasting paint colors are used, but you could also try using similar paint colors for a more subtle effect.

YOU WILL NEED

Protective gloves
Paintbrushes
Matte latex paint in two colors
Silicon-carbide abrasive paper
Crackle-glaze medium
Hairdryer (optional)

01 Use a paintbrush to apply two coats of matte latex paint, letting the first coat dry before applying the second, and sanding between coats.

02 Lightly sand all over to give a smooth finish.

03 Use a clean paintbrush to apply the crackle-glaze medium liberally. A thick coat of crackle-glaze will produce larger cracks than a thin coat. Leave to dry, following the manufacturer's instructions.

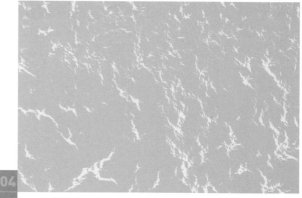

04 Use a clean brush to apply the top coat of latex paint, using short, quick brushstrokes. Do not overbrush the paint because the crackle-glaze medium will be activated as soon as the top coat has been applied and overbrushing can cause it to lift. Let dry.

APPROPRIATE SURFACES

For this finish the surface is painted solidly, so it is perfect for MDF or a wood that does not have an interesting grain or color. Real wood in poor condition would also be a good candidate for painting.

PREPARATION

Preparation is very important for this technique; shortcuts may result in surface chipping if the crackle-glaze does not adhere. Make sure the surface is smooth and dust free, and seal with shellac sanding sealer.

FINISHING

Protect the finish with at least two coats of water-based varnish or the medium recommended by the crackle-glaze manufacturer.

DRYING TIMES

• Allow at least four hours for the latex paint to dry before applying the crackle-glaze medium.
• Crackle-glaze drying times vary, so follow the manufacturer's recommendations.
• Allow to dry overnight before varnishing.

A SELECTION OF CRACKLE-GLAZE FINISHES

1 White base coat and pink top coat.
2 Brown base coat and pink top coat.
3 Dark green base coat and yellow top coat.

• Experiment with combinations of color and shade. Some colors look best as the top coat; others, especially the brighter colors, work better underneath.
• Bold, obvious cracking is not necessarily the most attractive; smaller cracks displaying a deeper base color can be just as interesting and offer a more varied, realistic imitation of natural aging. Experiment with applications of thin and thick layers of crackle-glaze to decide on the quality of cracking you wish to use.

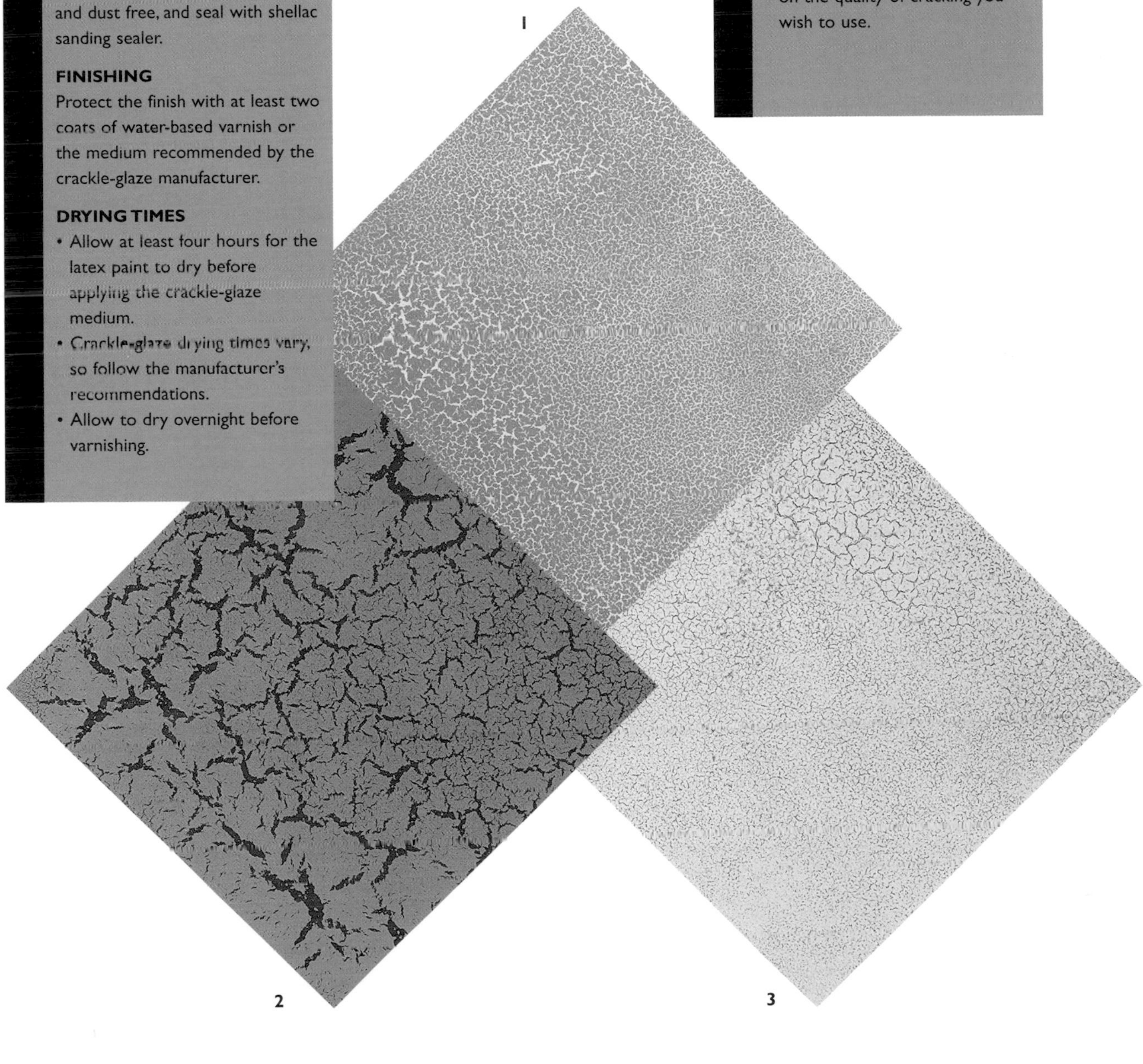

1

2

3

SEE ALSO
Preparation, pages 24–71
Staining wood, page 62
Wax finishes, page 78
French polishing, page 84

DISTRESSED FINISHES

Distressing techniques are used to "age" contemporary furniture or new components of antique pieces. To imitate the effects of age on natural wood you can use hard objects to make dents in the wood that are then filled with stain, or rub stain selectively onto areas of furniture to produce the highlights and dark patches of wear.

YOU WILL NEED

Bag of nuts and bolts
Water-based stain
Paintbrush
Protective gloves
Cotton cloth
Shellac sanding sealer
Metal container (can)
Alcohol stains
Mop brush
White polish (shellac)
Polishing pad (see page 85)
Fine steel wool
Furniture wax

Without holding back on distressing the surface as a whole, concentrate on the areas likely to suffer with time. Legs get bashed regularly, as do edges and tabletops. The simplest guide is to look at old furniture and try to imitate the markings. Mass-produced reproduction furniture often exhibits distressing that looks too systematic, since it follows a pattern, having been done by machine. So aim to keep the effect as natural as possible, and practice first on some scrap wood or even on a rejected piece of furniture that is beyond repair.

DISTRESSING NATURAL WOOD

This distressing is done with hard objects, such as bags of nuts and bolts, bicycle chains, and hammers, often softened by cloth. Water marks can be reproduced by using a cup with hot water smeared on the bottom. When distressing, make sure the marks are deep enough to break the fibers thoroughly, so they will take plenty of water-based stain. This makes the dents look even darker, as if they have collected dirt over the years.

01 Use a bag of nuts and bolts to make bruises and dents on the surface. The contents need to be heavy enough to do some damage. Make sure you move the bag around in a random motion; mass-produced reproduction furniture can be identified by a regular pattern. Concentrate on edges and legs.

02 Once the surface has been distressed, apply a dark shade of water-based stain. Use plenty of stain, keeping it wet as you manipulate it around the piece. Rub the stain into the damaged fibers of the bruises and dents so that they show up darker. Leave any odd splashes to simulate splashed marks made over the years, but rub the stain off the corners and moldings, as would happen with time.

03 When the stain has dried, seal the surface with a shellac sanding sealer, wiping it across the surface with a soft cloth, using straight strokes along the grain. The idea is to seal in the stain, and not to build up a finish. Ensure that the coat of sealer is even.

USEFUL INFORMATION

APPROPRIATE SURFACES

Any piece can be given an antique finish. However, an antique or distressed finish is obviously inappropriate for contemporary furniture.

PREPARATION

Make sure the surface is smooth and dust free. When preparing the surface, bruises and knocks can of course be ignored, but do not be tempted to ignore machining marks, which will betray the youth of the piece.

DRYING TIMES

- Allow 24 hours for water-based stains to dry before applying further coats or other finishes.
- Alcohol stains take only five minutes to dry.
- White polish will dry in one hour, but leave overnight before applying further finishes.
- Allow oil stains to dry for 30 to 40 minutes before rubbing.

HINTS AND TIPS

- The distressing pattern will not look natural if it is too regular.
- Do not distress an existing finish. Pieces must be stripped back first.
- Use deliberate strokes when distressing.
- Rub in the stain well.
- Look at antique furniture to see how and where it wears.

04

Many old pieces have ring marks from alcohol on glasses or hot water under cups and mugs. To imitate such a mark, fill a metal container with hot water and wet the bottom. Leave this on the surface for five to ten minutes to make a dark ring.

05

If the stain has not been sufficient to give the piece a color that reproduces the effects of aging, mix alcohol stains with white polish and apply with a mop brush. Cover the whole surface liberally with color and rub into the wood, to produce a darker finish. Try to produce a slightly opaque color mix.

06

After the color has dried, apply a coat of white polish using a polishing pad (see pages 85–87). Work up a body until a finish just short of full grain has been produced. Start with a circular pattern, moving across the surface. Finish with straight strokes following the grain.

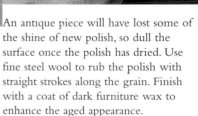

07

An antique piece will have lost some of the shine of new polish, so dull the surface once the polish has dried. Use fine steel wool to rub the polish with straight strokes along the grain. Finish with a coat of dark furniture wax to enhance the aged appearance.

This subtly aged mahogany panel can now sit more comfortably in a room full of antiques.

RUBBED FINISH

A rubbed finish is used to simulate the effects of age on a piece of furniture or paneling, by rubbing stain selectively to produce the highlights and dark patches of wear. The idea is to remove the finish from those areas that over the years would be worn away. The tops of beads on moldings and the edges and corners of chairs and tables are, for example, particularly liable to wear. Lighter areas will also appear at the center of panels, seats, or chair backs.

YOU WILL NEED

Protective gloves
Cotton cloth
Water-based stain
Silicon-carbide abrasive paper
Oil stain
Fine steel wool
Polishing pad (see page 85)
White polish (shellac)
Furniture wax

01 Damp down the surface to raise the grain. Use a cloth to apply a dark water-based stain—in this case Van Dyke brown, which penetrates well and can be worked into corners and crevices to give a darker color there. Rub the stain into the moldings.

USEFUL INFORMATION

APPROPRIATE SURFACES
Rubbing is most commonly done on oak and mock Jacobean furniture—but there is no reason why it cannot be used on other furniture or on items made from other woods.

DRYING TIMES
Leave the rubbed oil stain overnight before polishing.

02 Wipe off surplus stain with a clean cloth and leave to dry. Sand lightly and overstain using a dark oil stain. Apply more stain to the areas of the object that are likely to be less affected by wear, such as inside corners. Leave for 30 to 40 minutes to dry.

HINTS AND TIPS

- The gradual shading of a rubbed effect can be difficult to achieve, but is important. Remove the stain gradually by rubbing in progressive stages.
- Do not make sharp lines—the rubbed effect must blend in subtly.
- Make sure the surface is smooth at each stage.

03

Form some fine steel wool into a pad that fits in the hand. Use this to rub off the stain in the worn areas. Start from the center of a rail or panel and work toward the corners. Rub off more stain in the center than in the corners, blending gradually toward them.

04

Finish with white polish applied using a polishing pad (see page 85). Leave to dry and continue polishing, but do not build up a high-gloss finish, which would be inappropriate on antique furniture. Once the polish has dried, use fine steel wool to dull the finish, to create a semi-gloss effect, always following the grain. Apply a wax finish with a soft cloth to bring out the color and add depth.

SEE ALSO
Preparation, pages 24–71
Varnishing, page 80

GILDING

The term gilding refers not just to gold, but encompasses the application of all metal leaves and powders, from silver and platinum to bronze, aluminum, and gold-colored alloys. It has been used as a form of decoration for thousands of years, but the methods of application have barely changed. Gilding can be a difficult art to master, taking much skill and practice, but the methods described here should prove relatively easy.

Traditionally, there are two varieties of true gilding—water-based and oil-based. Water gilding is highly delicate and can be ruined by dampness. It is also a far more difficult technique than oil, involving only water with a minute addition of glue as an adhesive, and it cannot be used with patent metal leaf. Oil gilding—also known as mordant gilding—is easier to undertake, much more adaptable, and less vulnerable, so is the technique used here.

GOLD SIZE

The glue used in oil gilding is called gold size and is available from craft and art stores. Sizes are often quoted in terms of their drying time. Drying time is important because the quicker the surface dries, the less danger there is from dust or pollution. However, the slower the drying time, the more time you have to work and the better the gleam.

The size should be decanted from the tin into a clean paint kettle or container with a wire or thread tightly strung across the top. This strike wire will allow the size that is wiped off the brush to drain back into the container without forming bubbles. Only decant the amount of size needed for the job. More can be added if need be, but once the size has been decanted it should not be returned to the original tin.

Once the size has been applied, wait until it is almost dry before applying the metal leaf or powder. If the size is still soft, the leaf will be vulnerable to marks and will be dull. It is advisable to test the size's drying time on a spare board before you begin work on your actual piece.

USEFUL INFORMATION

APPROPRIATE SURFACES
For this finish the surface is solidly covered, so it is perfect for MDF or a wood that does not have an interesting grain or color.

PREPARATION
Ensure that the surface is flat and free from dust before applying size, so fill the grain and remove any dust. Absorbent wood can be sealed with shellac sanding sealer. An undercoat can also be applied.

FINISHING
It is a good idea to protect your work with an oil-based varnish.

After antiquing gold leaf you can apply a varnish if you would like a sheen, but protection is not necessary because natural wear and tear will add to the effect.

DRYING TIMES
Gold size has various drying times, so follow the manufacturer's recommendations and test the size on a spare or unseen surface.

Allow the gilding to dry overnight before varnishing.

LOOSE-LEAF GILDING

If you want to use loose-leaf for gilding you will need some specialist equipment. Before you begin, dust your gilders' cushion, knife, and tip with gilders' whiting, using a pounce bag to prevent the gold leaf from sticking. The leaves can be placed on the cushion as required. The size of the leaf depends on the surface to be gilded, but you should allow a reasonable overlap.

YOU WILL NEED

Gold size and application brush
Gold or metal leaf
Gilders' cushion
Gilders' knife
Gilders' tip
Gilders' whiting
Pounce bag
Gilders' mop

01 Apply the gold size smoothly and evenly so that the whole area is ready for gilding at roughly the same time. Allow the size to tack off.

02 Cut the leaf to size using the gilders' knife on the cushion. Hold the knife blade flat against the leaf and keep an even contact with the surface. Cut with one pull. Flatten and smooth the leaf by turning it with the knife and blowing to remove the wrinkles.

03 Prepare the gilders' tip to transfer the leaves to the sized surface by brushing it over your cheek. With enough oil for adhesion, lift the leaf from the cushion, remembering that the tip should be smaller than the cut leaves.

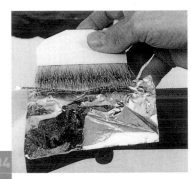

04 Apply the leaf to the sized surface in a gentle down-up movement. Try to deposit the leaf onto the surface in one smooth action. Continue applying the leaves in the same way, overlapping them by 3⁄16 in. (5 mm), until you have laid six leaves.

05 Press the gold against the surface with a lightly used gilders' mop. Wrinkles will appear, but will disappear when the surface is brushed clean.

06 Gently brush the excess loose leaf—known as skewings—off the surface, catching them in a pot or on the cushion. The small faults that appear as you progress can be mended by pressing the skewings into them. Use the mop to press down the gold and remove excess leaf. Continue until you have covered the surface.

PATENT-LEAF GILDING

Patent leaf has a transparent tissue backing that allows you to position the leaf accurately, and manipulation of the leaf is done by hand rather than with a knife and tip, so it is easier to handle. If the leaf needs cutting, use long-bladed scissors or a scalpel in a single movement, to avoid tearing. When placing the gold, make sure that you have enough elbow and wrist support to prevent undue movement.

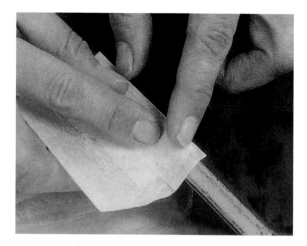

Apply the gold size in the same way as for loose leaf and allow it to tack off (see page 117). Lift the patent leaf from its book by holding the backing sheet with both hands and place the leaf onto the tacky size. Hold the backing paper with one hand and stroke the leaf into position with the fingers of your other hand. Gently remove the transparent backing to expose the gilded surface. The next leaf should overlap the previous by ³⁄₁₆ in. (5 mm). Continue to apply sheets of leaf in the same way. When you have completed the area, use a mop to dust off unwanted debris. Use discarded leaf still attached to the backing paper to fill in any gaps.

GILDING WITH POWDER

When working with fine-ground powders it is advisable to wear a dust mask.

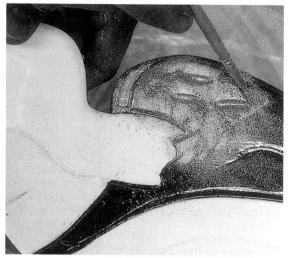

Apply the size as for loose leaf and allow it to tack off (see page 117). Cover the sticky size with the dry powder, using a soft-haired mop to work it into all the details. When the size has dried for at least an hour, gently remove the loose powder, using a soft cloth.

LEAF AND POWDERS

Metal leaf and powder can both be used to add a metallic sheen to wood or MDF surfaces. Metal leaves usually impart a brighter sheen, while powders can be used for a solid but soft effect. Patent metal leaves, whether gold, silver, bronze, copper, Dutch metal (imitation gold), or aluminum, are attached to a backing sheet that makes them easier to handle than the traditional loose leaf, which requires specialist equipment to cut and use and can be difficult to control. Metal powders range from pale gold to dark bronze. Application works well on small areas and is best achieved in a draft-free environment.

YOU WILL NEED

Item gilded with gold leaf
Oil-based varnish
Varnish brush
Fine steel wool
Burnt sienna or burnt umber
   oil-based glaze
Cotton cloth
Open-weave cloth
Mineral spirits

ANTIQUING GOLD

Antiquing is a simulated aging that can soothe a piece into its surroundings. Gold leaf is often antiqued, especially when applied to a classical design, where it may otherwise look too new and bright. The usual medium uses an oil-based glaze mixed with burnt umber or burnt sienna artists' oil paints (see page 96), which imparts a rich glow and is bold enough to reduce the gold's power while retaining a warmth that enhances the piece.

01 Protect the gilded surface with a thin coat of oil-based varnish and allow to dry. Rub over the surface with fine steel wool to give an impression of wear. Concentrate on proud surfaces, edges, and areas more prone to wear and tear.

02 Mix a strongly colored burnt sienna or burnt umber oil-based glaze— here burnt sienna is used. Apply the glaze liberally over the area with a cloth, taking care to penetrate all the details of the work. Allow the glaze a little time to adhere.

03 Using an open-weave cloth, dab and rub the glaze over the entire surface. This technique removes some of the glaze and ensures that all crevices and hollows have been thoroughly covered.

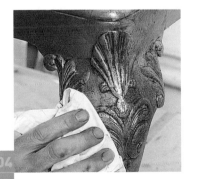

04 Use a clean cotton cloth to remove the remaining glaze. In some instances it may be necessary to use a little mineral spirits on the cloth to produce highlights.

05 The antiqued effect warms and softens the gilding; the finished object glows rather than standing out brashly.

06 When a heavier antique finish is needed, drag the glaze over the moldings and carvings using an open-weave cloth and only the high points will appear as clean gold. The remainder will vary in tone according to its position.

SEE ALSO
Preparation, pages 24–71
Varnishing, page 80

LIMING

Liming is a very similar effect to pickling (see page 122), but originates from a much earlier technique. Liming dates back to sixteenth-century Europe, when an unction containing the very corrosive slaked lime was applied to furniture and paneling to prevent worm and beetle infestation. Trapped in the pores of the open-grained timber, the white paste not only repelled the pests but also produced a pleasing visual effect. This became increasingly popular, reaching its height in the seventeenth century.

YOU WILL NEED

Wire brush
Liming paste
Paintbrushes
Cotton cloth
Shellac sanding sealer
Very fine abrasive paper

Open-grained wood is still the best choice for this effect, and you will only need to give it a light brushing with a wire brush prior to treatment. Close-grained woods will need more work with the brush. Once the grain has been readied in this way, you can apply a liming paste.

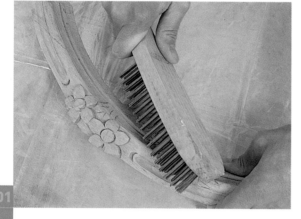

01 Open the grain by rubbing the surface with a stiff wire brush, using straight strokes along the grain. Try to open the grain evenly, and not more deeply in some areas than in others. Check the results regularly against the light, making sure the whole surface has been worked with the wire brush.

02 Liming paste is a combination of wax and white pigments, and can be bought ready-mixed. Use a paintbrush to apply the paste. Work across the grain, making sure all the pores are filled. Try not to use too much paste at any one time.

03 Before the paste dries, use a clean dry cloth to remove the excess from the surface of the piece, leaving it in the pores and open grain.

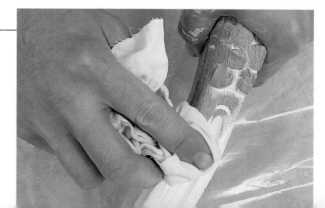

USEFUL INFORMATION

APPROPRIATE SURFACES

Open-grained timbers, especially oak, elm, and ash. Close-grained woods can also be used but will need more work with the wire brush before applying the liming paste. This technique is ideal for chairs, tables, picture frames, kitchen furniture and fittings, paneling, staircases, and restored furniture.

PREPARATION

Make sure the piece is sanded smooth and free from dust or grease. If you need to stain the piece, use a water-based stain before liming, and seal with a shellac sanding sealer. Leave overnight to ensure that the sealer is thoroughly dry and hard before rubbing in the liming paste—otherwise the stain can be worked away, resulting in a patchy effect.

FINISHING

Protect the effect with a clear varnish. Varnishing brings the finish alive, revealing how the grain has picked up the white flecks of the liming paste.

DRYING TIME

Leave liming paste to dry overnight before finishing off.

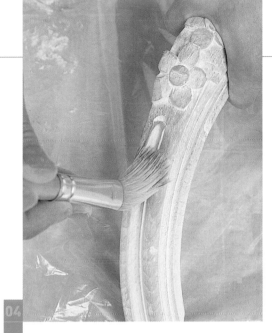

04

Leave the paste to dry overnight, then apply a coat of shellac sanding sealer with a paintbrush and allow to dry.

05

Sand the piece with a very fine abrasive paper to create an ultra-smooth finish for varnishing.

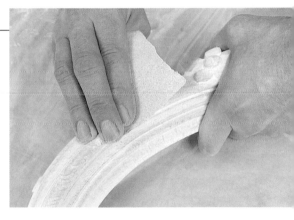

SEE ALSO
Preparation, pages 24–71
Varnishing, page 80

PICKLING

This effect dates back to a finish called pickle pine, which evolved in the late nineteenth century. At the time, paint was commonly used to conceal the cheap construction of much of the pine, or "deal," furniture to be found in the servants' quarters and among the less well-off. But the emergence of the Arts and Crafts movement fueled a fashion for natural wood, and stripping painted pine became increasingly popular.

YOU WILL NEED

Paintbrushes
White latex paint
Cotton cloth
Fine abrasive paper

The stripping was a highly dangerous treatment undertaken with nitric acid. This left the wood looking aged and ashen, with white or gray remnants of paint and gesso clinging to the crevices. In some cases, the wood lost its color and resembled driftwood. In others, the color was darkened.

This "soft-on-the-eye" effect (which came about by accident) was so admired that soon a technique was developed to apply it to new furniture. This involved bleaching and staining the wood, followed by filling the grain with a white or gray paint or paste. By the 1930s the effect was being used extensively, and cheap shortcuts were replacing the genuine technique for treating new wood.

Today the effect can be achieved with little risk because no acid is used. Purists may view it with some disdain, but its pale chalky demeanor and the ease with which it enables a piece to fit into a color scheme have guaranteed pickling, like liming, a resurgence in popularity.

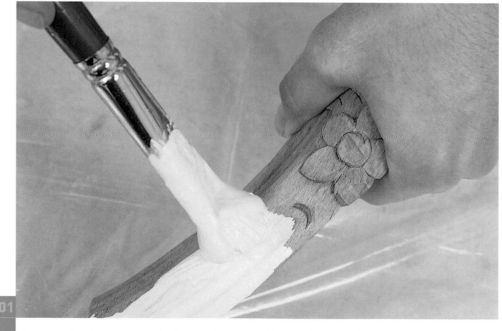

01 Use a paintbrush to apply white latex paint to a small area of the sealed surface, otherwise the paint will dry before you have a chance to wipe it off. Make sure every nook and cranny is covered.

USEFUL INFORMATION

APPROPRIATE SURFACES
Best suited to pale woods with plenty of detailing and molding, since the white paint is naturally trapped by crevices and corners.

PREPARATION
The piece to be finished should be in a raw state, and free of grease and grime. If the wood is very pale you can stain at this stage to provide some contrast with the top coat. The surface should be sealed with a shellac sanding sealer.

FINISHING
Protect the finish with one or two coats of clear varnish.

DRYING TIME
Allow at least four hours for the latex paint to dry.

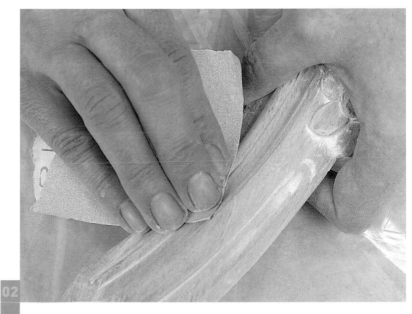

02 Use a cotton cloth to wipe the paint off the majority of the surface—only the detailing will readily retain the paint. Continue to apply and wipe off the paint on small areas at a time.

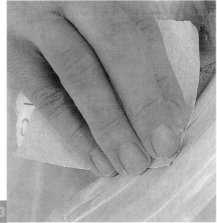

03 When the piece is dry, sand it with fine abrasive paper, remembering to work with the grain.

SEE ALSO
Preparation, pages 24–71
Varnishing, page 80

STIPPLING

Stippling is probably the simplest of paint effects to produce on timber and fiberboard. An oil–based glaze (see page 96) is applied over a dry undercoat and a stippling brush is then bounced across the surface with a pouncing movement, producing a fine pepper-like, orange-peel finish. The subtlety of this effect is enhanced by the glowing transparency of the glaze.

YOU WILL NEED

Undercoat
Paintbrushes
Silicon-carbide abrasive paper
Oil-based glaze
Stippling brush
Cotton cloth
Open-weave cloth

Stippling brushes are available from decorating suppliers and are designed to produce this distinct, ordered pattern, although upholstery foam, sponges, and paper towels also work well.

The background color is a matter of choice, so experiment with pastel and darker colors. Matching colors, only distinguished by a slight difference in tone, may be most suitable—but startling results can be achieved with contrasting hues.

HINTS AND TIPS

- Practice on scrap board and test effects before stippling.
- Vary the way you dab the stippling brush for a random effect.
- Try using different materials for stippling—almost anything will do.
- Any accidental damage will be very evident in a stippled finish. If damage occurs and the surface is still wet, reapply glaze quickly to the affected area and restipple. If, however, the glaze has begun to dry, or tack off, a renewed application of glaze will react against the tacky glaze and worsen the fault. If you can live with the fault, leave it. If not, remove the glaze with a cloth and mineral spirits and allow the surface to dry for at least two hours before reapplication.

01
Paint on an undercoat, allow to dry, and lightly sand. Brush on an oil-based glaze. When finishing an edged surface, such as this tabletop, apply the glaze first to the edge and then to the larger top.

02
To lay off the glaze, wipe the brush on the side of the can and use long, even, light strokes to reduce and eliminate brushmarks. Do not allow to dry.

APPROPRIATE SURFACES

For this finish the surface is painted solidly so it is perfect for MDF or a wood that does not have an interesting grain or color. Real wood in poor condition would also be a good candidate for painting. By far the best substrate for stippling is MDF, which is smooth and takes finishes perfectly.

PREPARATION

A standard stipple requires top-quality preparation: the effect is so finely textured that any flaw stands out like a sore thumb. Make sure the wood is smooth and dust free. Unlike MDF, timber and chipboard need filling with plaster of Paris before stippling. Absorbent wood can be sealed with shellac sanding sealer.

FINISHING

It is a good idea to protect your work with a matte or semi-gloss varnish.

DRYING TIMES

- Let undercoat dry overnight.
- Let the glaze dry for 24 to 48 hours before varnishing.

- When working with oil-based glazes, do so in a well-ventilated area.
- Spread out cloths that have become saturated with glaze and leave to dry before disposing of them. Wet cloths have a low flash point and can combust.

03

Hold a stippling brush firmly and dab it into the still-wet glaze to remove areas of glaze and produce the speckled finish. Maintain an even action as you move around the surface, ensuring that the pressure of each dab is similar. Try not to go over one area more often than others. Stipple the edge of a tabletop first, because this cannot be done without overlapping the top.

04

Stipple the top, holding the brush at right angles and allowing the bristles to act like springs. Remember to wipe the brush occasionally with a cloth to remove the glaze. Step away from the area to check the overall look, and jab the brush lightly at any dark patches.

05

Use a piece of open-weave cloth wrapped around your finger to achieve a dragged look over any molding.

MARBLE EFFECT

The most obvious reason for creating a marbled effect is the desire to imitate real marble, and in grand period houses it is not uncommon to find outstanding examples of marbling that are difficult to distinguish from the real thing.

To achieve the effect, oil-based glazes (see page 96) are applied over an undercoat and manipulated with brushes while still wet. Look at some examples of real marble to help you mix the desired color of glaze, and make sure the edges of a piece of furniture are treated in the same way as the rest of the piece to make it look like solid marble.

For this example, we have chosen to replicate an Egyptian green marble. This rich dark green marble is often used on pilasters and plinths, but its intricate detail and luxurious quality make it appropriate for smaller items such as tabletops and inlays.

YOU WILL NEED

Black undercoat
Paintbrushes
Silicon-carbide abrasive paper
Toothbrush or stencil brush
Vermilion oil-based glaze
Terre-verte oil-based glaze
Artists' writing brush
Newspaper
White undercoat
Mineral spirits
Sword brush
Badger-hair softening brush
Artists' 00 brush
Cotton cloth

USEFUL INFORMATION

APPROPRIATE SURFACES
For this finish the surface is painted solidly, so it is perfect for MDF or a wood that does not have an interesting grain or color. Real wood in poor condition would also be a good candidate for painting.

PREPARATION
Make sure the wood is smooth and dust free. Fill the grain if necessary. You may want to continue the marbling around corners for three-dimensional realism, so make sure the edges are cleaned up and that holes are filled and sanded flat.

FINISHING
A clear semi-gloss, oil-based varnish makes a good finish. Use fine silicon-carbide paper to smooth the surface between coats.

DRYING TIMES
Let undercoat dry overnight. Let the glazes dry for 24 to 48 hours before varnishing.

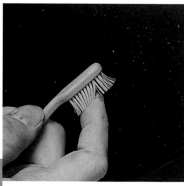

01 Paint on a black undercoat and sand when dry. Using a toothbrush or stencil brush, spatter vermilion glaze onto the black ground and allow it to become tacky.

02 Load an artists' writing brush with terre-verte oil-based glaze and twist the brush between finger and thumb to roll the glaze onto the ground.

HINTS AND TIPS

If the badger-hair softening brush is not kept clean, it can smudge the effect.

HEALTH AND SAFETY

Always work in a well-ventilated area when using oil-based glazes. Spread out cloths that have become saturated with glaze and leave to dry before disposing of them. Wet cloths have a low flash point and can combust.

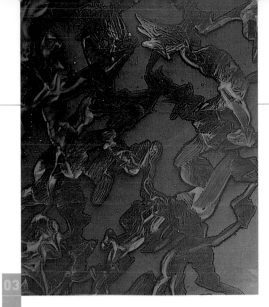

03 Roll the brush this way and that, while drawing it over the surface until about three-quarters of the area is covered.

04 Soften the effect by crushing newspaper into a pad and dabbing it over the surface.

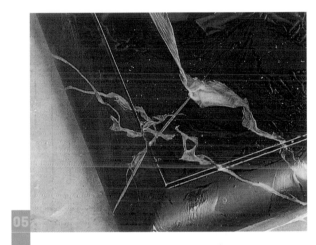

05 While the ground is still wet, apply white undercoat thinned with mineral spirits using a sword brush. Again, roll the brush between finger and thumb, and use its flat, tapered shape to produce wide and narrow vein lines. Make all painting strokes toward the body, bringing the width and the heel of the brush into play when a broad vein is required, and the tip and edge of the brush for a thin vein.

06 When the initial veins are in, soften them with a badger-hair softening brush. Lightly brush the glaze with short strokes, just touching the surface, to blend the veins in with the background color. There must be no brushmarks left on the surface. The softening gives a smoky effect, and creates the illusion that the vein is a little way under the surface.

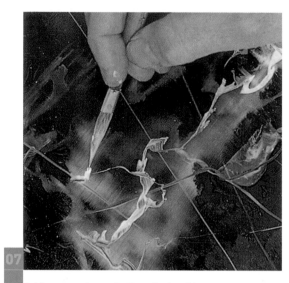

IMITATING MARBLE TILES

Real marble is usually positioned in panels, like tiles, with thin lines between them. You may want to imitate this pattern, in which case paint dark lines in a grid formation. Marble tiles vary in size, but are often about 12–15 in. (300–375 mm) square. Using a straightedge, draw on the grid before marbling the area. The tiles need not necessarily all be the same, and an interesting effect can be achieved by altering the color and grain of the marble.

07 Add more veins as in Step 5, sketching over the top of an earlier vein.

08 Continue to add veins and soften them, following Steps 5–6. Here you can see the gradual build-up of fine, straight crack veins that run at right angles to the original trend.

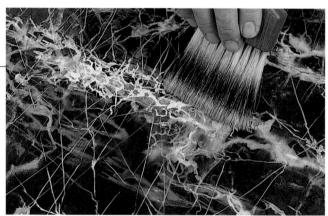

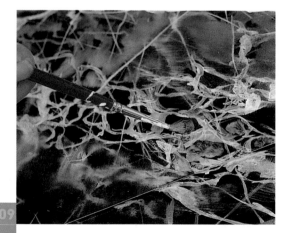

09 Pick out some of the small plates created as the white veins break up the surface using the vermilion glaze on an artists' 00 brush.

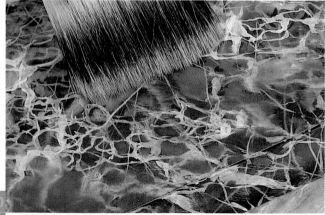

10 Soften the vermilion plates using the badger-hair brush. Softening is crucial to successful marbling and the bristles should hardly touch the surface.

HINTS AND TIPS

- Have a good look at real marble before attempting to create any marble effect.
- Always practice on scrap material first.
- Apply thin, not heavy, layers of color.
- Wash off failed effects with mineral spirits and start again.
- Always mix enough glaze to finish the job.
- Carry effects around edges to give an illusion of solidity.
- When experimenting with creating your own marble effect, use pale colors at first, and try blending them together, as if building up layers. Look closely at real marble to see what you are attempting to copy. When you understand how to manipulate the glaze, move on to more dramatic marble effects, using stronger colors.
- Rag-rolled borders (see pages 130–131) enhance the effect and make it more interesting.

11 Only a clean brush will produce a good-quality finish, so clean the bristles regularly with a dry cloth.

12 The completed surface shows a swirling, frothy network of veins intersected by fine lines.

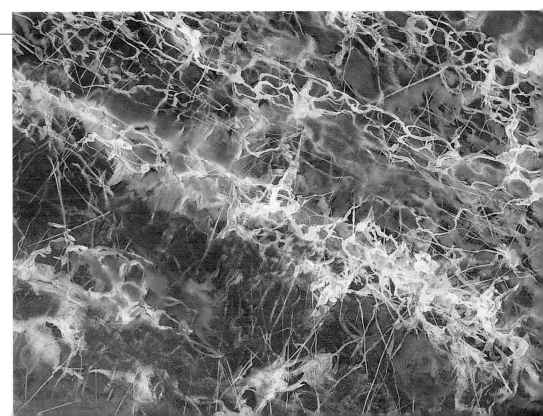

SEE ALSO
Preparation, pages 24–71
Varnishing, page 80

RAG-ROLLING

A traditional method of creating a mottled paint effect on furniture and paneling is to roll the surface with rags dipped in oil-based glaze (see page 96). Once the glaze is dry, further applications can be made for contrasting color.

YOU WILL NEED

Undercoat
Paintbrush
Silicon-carbide abrasive paper
Low-tack masking tape
Cotton cloth
Oil-based glaze in two colors
Badger-hair softening brush

When the paint-effects revolution ignited in the 1980s, rag-rolling was among the most widely used techniques. Its popularity remains, but a softer, more gentle approach is now favored. Today, the use of subtle, close color combinations lends an understated, contemporary twist to this finish.

01 Paint on an undercoat and allow to dry before lightly sanding. Use low-tack masking tape to mask off areas not to be rag-rolled. Cut a large cotton cloth into three pieces. Partially dip one piece of cloth into the first glaze, taking care not to saturate it. Work the glaze through the cloth, until the entire cloth has absorbed some of the glaze. Roll the cloth into a sausage shape. Starting at the bottom and using arcing movements, roll the cloth up the surface, repeating until the entire surface is evenly covered with ragging marks. Use a new rag when necessary.

02 To soften and blend the effect of the rag-rolling, lightly dust a badger-hair softening brush over the still-wet glaze in all directions. Leave until thoroughly dry.

USEFUL INFORMATION

APPROPRIATE SURFACES

For this finish the surface is painted solidly, so it is perfect for MDF or a wood that does not have an interesting grain or color. Real wood in poor condition would also be a good candidate for painting. From a furniture-maker's point of view, MDF is the best substrate on which to work.

PREPARATION

Make sure the surface is smooth and dust free. Absorbent wood can be sealed with shellac sanding sealer.

FINISHING

Protect with one to three coats of matte or semi-gloss water-based varnish since polyurethane or oil varnish will alter the color of the paint.

DRYING TIMES

• Let undercoat dry overnight.
• Leave the glaze for a day or two to dry thoroughly, before varnishing.

HINTS AND TIPS

• Try out color combinations on scrap wood before rag-rolling.
• Do not overload the rag with glaze—if it is dripping or sodden, this means that it is oversaturated, and a new rag should be used for best effect.
• Always roll in arced lines rather than straight lines, so that the ragging marks are irregular. Recrunching the cloth periodically will ensure that the same markings are not repeated.
• Only attempt small areas at a time.
• It is easy to let the color and effect vary over large areas. Try to keep it even and constant throughout—especially when, after working round a large piece, the first edge meets up with the last.

03 Using a new rag, take up the second glaze and lightly roll it over the previously rolled surface. Again, blend using the softening brush. Dab extra glaze onto any uneven patches. Soften once more, then allow to dry thoroughly.

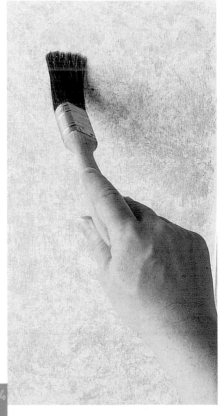

04 To finish, apply three coats of either matte or semi gloss water-based varnish, allowing each coat to dry before applying the next. Do not use oil-based varnish because this will yellow over time.

04

SPRAY FINISHES

At the beginning of the nineteenth century, as mass production of furniture grew, so demand increased for finishes that would be easy and quick to apply, hard-wearing, and maintenance-free. As a result, a whole new industry evolved, devoted to simulating traditional finishes. The scope and range of modern finishes is as wide and varied, and the preparation of the surface every bit as important as for hand-applied finishes.

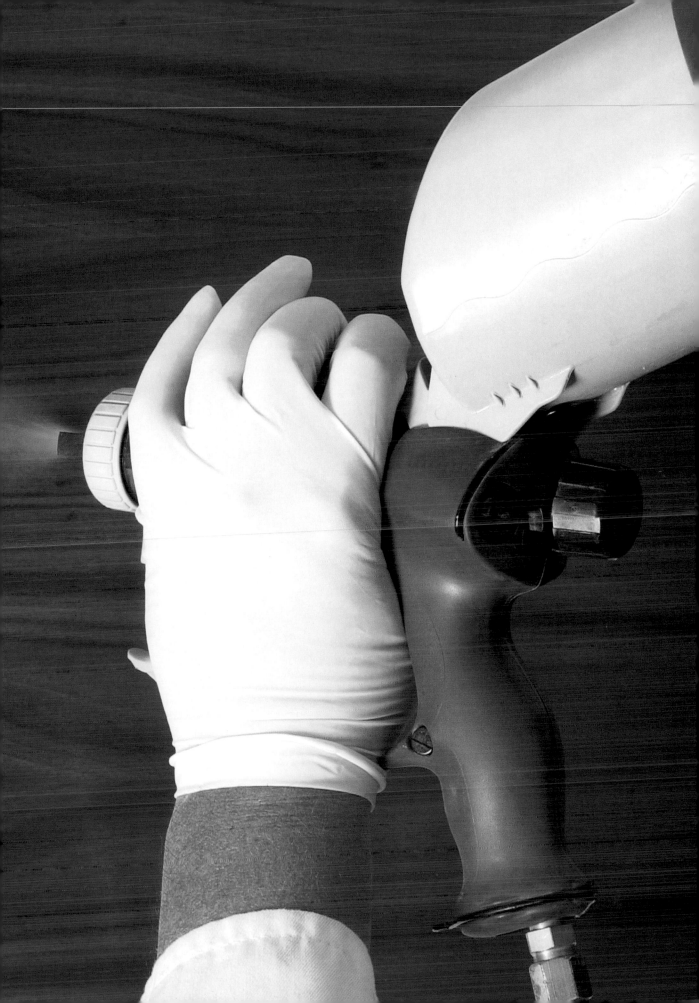

SPRAY GUNS

The principal feature that distinguishes the various types of spray gun is the way the finish is held and then passed to the nozzle for atomizing with compressed air. There are basically three options—and unless bulk spraying with a pressure-feed gun is required, the choice is limited to gravity-feed and suction-feed guns. For small jobs such as stenciling the range can be extended to aerosols, but they are rarely used by professional finishers, except for touching up damaged spray finishes on site.

YOU WILL NEED

A gravity-feed gun
A suction-feed gun
A small retouch gun
Air regulator
Breathing equipment
Face mask with air flow
Masking tape

Convenience, economy, and the types of finish to be used are the criteria to consider when choosing a spray gun. For the small workshop, gravity-feed guns are normally the most convenient. They are easy to handle, economical (as small quantities can be mixed for short jobs), and suitable for most finishes.

Gravity-feed guns are susceptible to clogging and slow flow when spraying heavy paints because of their high solid content, especially those that produce a metallic effect. Suction-feed guns are better for such work, but are generally not as convenient to use because the underslung reservoir makes them unwieldy. However, they only need small quantities of finish at a time.

Each of these guns (with perhaps the exception of aerosols) produces the smooth finish associated with spraying, so long as they are maintained properly (see page 137) and the materials and workpiece are thoroughly prepared. Aerosols are more difficult to use because they cannot be adjusted and the material is not atomized as consistently.

USEFUL INFORMATION

Other than heavy paints with a high solid content, any finish can be used in a gravity-feed gun.

COMMON PROBLEMS
If the flow is too slow for atomizing, the finish is probably too heavy and a suction-feed gun is needed.

GRAVITY-FEED SPRAY GUNS

Most woodworkers wanting to kit up their workshop for spraying are likely to buy a gravity-feed spray system. Gravity guns are simple and easy to use. The finish is mixed and stored in a cup that screws onto the top of the gun. The cup takes about 1 pt (550 ml), which is ample for spraying both sides of a 6 ft (2 m) tabletop with one coat of finish.

In use, the finish flows down into the gun and out of the nozzle. Then the finish is atomized by air blown through small holes (called atomizing holes) in the air cap, which surrounds the nozzle, and through the horn holes that stand proud on each side of the air cap. With the compressor working, the gun is constantly ready; but the compressed air will only flow when the trigger is squeezed. Squeezing the trigger opens the air valve and draws the needle away from the nozzle to let the finish out. However, the initial pressure on the trigger opens the air valve only a little, without allowing the finish to flow, thus ensuring that material does not drip out of the gun onto the workpiece without being atomized.

The beauty of the gravity-feed gun is that it is so easy to use. The cup does not get in the way as you spray, and you can work with small quantities of finish at a time.

HINTS AND TIPS

It is important not to run out of material midway through spraying a large surface because spray finishes dry within minutes and trying to spray a surface in stages can result in a patchy finish. There are few wood-finishing operations that will use up a full cup in one go—but always err on the side of generosity when measuring finish, so you do not run out at a critical moment. Equally, do not overfill the cup on a gravity-feed gun, as it can then spill finish over the piece as you spray, leaving conspicuous droplets that take time to flatten with abrasive.

When assembling the spray gun, make sure the small plastic filter at the bottom of the cup is in place, to stop dirt getting into the gun and blocking the nozzle.

If you are planning a long session of spraying with stain, mix plenty of stain in a larger container, because you will not be able to repeat the color exactly.

HINTS AND TIPS

Always select a good-quality spray gun. Buy the best you can afford. Try out the gun to see how it feels.

Always clean out after use, making sure the holes are not blocked. Lubricate all parts with general-use oil.

ANATOMY OF A GRAVITY-FEED SPRAY GUN

This gun is probably the best piece of equipment for anyone taking up spray finishing.

CUP
The cup stores the finish and screws into the top of the gun.

SPREAD ADJUSTER
This regulates the quantity of air flowing out of the horn holes in the cap and so changes the shape of the fan.

NEEDLE ADJUSTER
The needle restricts the amount of fluid flowing out of the gun.

AIR CAP
Air is blown through small holes in the air cap, atomizing the finish.

TRIGGER
Squeezing the trigger opens the air valve and draws a needle away from the nozzle to release the fluid.

HANDLE
Handle for gripping gun.

AIR FLOW ADJUSTER
This is adjusted to suit the material being sprayed—higher for thicker materials, lower for thin materials.

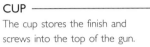

Each gun can be adapted to suit the needs of differing finishes by changing the set-up of air cap, nozzle, and needle. These are supplied in various shapes and sizes, with all sorts of hole configurations in the air cap. Each component is marked with a code, and manufacturers publish a chart to show which air cap should be used with which nozzle and needle for any particular finish. It is important to use the correct combination of parts.

Tell your supplier which finishes you expect to be spraying. The chances are that you will be able to use one versatile set-up for all wood finishes, but you may need a special air cap and nozzle for high viscosity finishes such as polyester and filling primers. Needles are usually standard, but check that you have one that is suitable.

The viscosity of a finish affects the set-up you choose. High viscosity finishes require a larger set-up.

Stains and polyurethanes have the lowest viscosity; and nitrocellulose the highest, though this depends on how much thinner is used (in order to produce a thin or thick coat). Whenever possible, use two thin applications rather than a single heavy coat.

SUCTION-FEED SPRAY GUNS

Suction-feed spray guns are broadly similar to gravity-feed types, but the finish is siphoned up from a canister slung below the gun. The nozzle of a suction-fed gun protrudes further through the air cap than on gravity-feed guns. As the air rushes out through the air cap, a vacuum is formed that sucks up the finish from the reservoir. Adjustments are much the same as on the other guns, though the set-up of nozzle, needle, and air cap is different.

One advantage of suction guns is that the reservoir can be larger than on a gravity gun. You therefore don't have to refill it as frequently, which saves time. It also helps when mixing the finish. As the canister holds that much more, mixing up in another container may be unnecessary. However, the size of the canister and the fact that it is often made from metal (rather than plastic as for gravity-feed guns) does make the gun heavy. Also, if you lose concentration, the canister tends to hit the surface and mark the finish.

Another advantage is that you can mix the finish in the canister before attaching it to the gun (whereas on a gravity gun the cup has to be screwed in place before it can be filled, which is less convenient).

When you look at a suction gun, you will notice that the pipe that picks up the finish from the canister is bent. This is a design feature. When the gun is tipped forward, as often happens while spraying, the pipe needs to point toward the front of the canister, to ensure that it sucks up finish and not air. If air is sucked up, then the finish is likely to be uneven.

Suction-feed guns are particularly suitable for spraying finishes with a high solid content, such as metallic paints, because heavy particles of finish tend to sink to the bottom of the reservoir, where they will not be sucked up—whereas they would be the first to drop into the workings of a gravity-feed gun, slowing the flow, or even block it up. Suction guns are, in fact, equally suitable for thin-flow coats. These are used when a thin final coat of finish is needed that will flow smoothly across the surface. They may have as much as 15 percent thinners content.

Suction-feed guns work well with any finish, but are particularly good for heavy metallic paints.

COMMON PROBLEMS
If the finish fluctuates and stutters when you are spraying, the reason may simply be that the suction pipe is not bent forward.

ANATOMY OF A SUCTION-FEED SPRAY GUN

This type of gun is recommended for spraying heavy pigmented finishes.

HINTS AND TIPS

Proper maintenance of a spray gun is essential. It will not work efficiently if any of the tiny air and fluid holes are even slightly blocked—and as modern spraying finishes dry very fast, this can happen quickly. Immediately after spraying is completed, pour any finish that remains in the cup into a waste container, for disposal at a toxic-waste disposal point.

Clean all parts of the gun with thinners, paying special attention to the holes in the air cap and nozzle, and take off the air cap and clean it thoroughly. Use a brush to clean the inside of the gun; and make sure that all holes are clear. Do not leave the gun to soak in thinners overnight. After cleaning, reassemble the gun and oil all moving parts.

HINTS AND TIPS

When fitting the canister to the gun, make sure the filter at the bottom of the pipe is in place and bent forward.

SPREAD ADJUSTER
This regulates the quantity of air flowing out of the horn holes in the cap and so changes the shape of the fan.

AIR CAP
Air is blown through small holes in the air cap, atomizing the finish.

NEEDLE ADJUSTER
The needle restricts the amount of fluid flowing out of the gun.

TRIGGER
Squeezing the trigger opens the air valve and draws a needle away from the nozzle to release the fluid.

HANDLE
Handle for gripping gun.

AIR FLOW ADJUSTER
This is adjusted to suit the material being sprayed— higher for thicker materials, lower for thin materials.

CUP
The cup stores the finish, and is carried below the gun.

COMPRESSORS AND AIR REGULATORS

For efficient spraying, air must be supplied to the gun at a constant pressure. It is also vital that the air is clean and dry. These requirements are met by two items of equipment: a compressor and an air regulator.

Compressors work by drawing air through a filter and pumping it, under pressure to a receiver tank, to the air regulator. The pump can be driven by a diesel or electric motor, but the cheaper ones plug into the mains and are much easier to maintain. The air regulator, which needs to be as near to the spray booth as possible, regulates the air pressure and extracts any moisture or oil. It incorporates a series of filters, and a meter to measure and adjust the air pressure.

When buying a compressor, the specifications to look for are the volume of air supplied and the maximum pressure that the compressor is capable of providing. Spray-gun manufacturers produce set-ups of air cap, needle, and nozzle to suit any air supply from 6–20 cubic ft (0.2–0.6 cubic m) per minute. For first-time buyers, they recommend a compressor that supplies 12 cubic ft (0.3 cubic m) per minute at 60 lb psi (4 bars) pressure. Once you have chosen a compressor, tell the spray-equipment supplier which kind you have selected and they will offer a set-up to suit your system.

While compressors can be bought or hired relatively cheaply from many manufacturers, it is best to purchase an air regulator from a spray-equipment supplier. It is important to buy a reliable one that will ensure a steady flow of compressed air. When you are spraying, there's nothing worse than a fluctuating air supply. If the air supply falters, the gun will splutter momentarily and will fail to atomize the material, allowing drops to fall to the surface.

Pressure pots and spray guns

HINTS AND TIPS

A drainage tap on the air regulator provides an outlet for collected moisture. Before and after each spraying session, open the tap to let out any water—otherwise it may percolate through to the gun and cause the finish to be ruined.

There is also a drainage tap on the compressor's receiver tank. When the compressor has been turned off, open this tap and let the water drain out (water tends to build up in the tank because air heats up and condenses it as it is subjected to pressure). The armature of the pump can burn out if it has to run against too much pressure—so if you are doing a long run of spraying, turn off the compressor at lunchtime and drain the tank before resuming work.

When buying your first spraying system, opt for a compressor that supplies about 12 cubic ft (0.3 cubic m) per minute at 60 lb psi (4 bars) pressure.

Try to position the air regulator as close to the spray gun as is conveniently possible.

HEALTH AND SAFETY

Do not open the drainage tap on the receiver tank while the pump is working or with the electricity supply turned on.

USEFUL INFORMATION

COMMON PROBLEMS
- If water or moisture gets to the surface, blisters and blooming are likely to form in the finish.
- If the air supply fluctuates and produces an uneven finish, check that the compressor and air regulator are drained and working properly.

THE SPRAY WORKSHOP

Very little equipment is needed in a spraying workshop—indeed, the less clutter the better, as it only collects dust. There are, however, a few important accessories that aid successful spraying, and, as always, natural light makes it so much easier to check the surface thoroughly.

SPRAY BOOTHS

The environment for spraying needs to be dust-free and well ventilated. Factories have sealed booths that provide a dedicated spraying area, with powerful extractor fans to clear the air in the booth of dangerous fumes.

You can build a small booth with a simple timber framework clad with thin plywood. Cut a hole in the back of the booth, and fit an extractor or fan to extract fumes from the workshop. Cover the hole with a fibrous filter to catch solids.

Line the sides of the booth with paper, so you can easily replace it when it gets coated with finish. It's vital to keep booths and spraying workshops clean because dust, besides marring sprayed finishes, is also a fire hazard. The extractor will pull dust toward it, so it is important to keep the area clean. Dampen the floor to trap dust.

When in the booth, never spray with the gun pointing away from the extractor—otherwise the spray will be diverted away from the area you are aiming at and may cover you instead. A revolving stand for the workpiece is therefore essential in a spray booth, so the piece can be turned and you don't have to move round it.

TURNTABLES

You can buy a turntable or make one of your own, by putting a platform on top of the swivel mechanism from an old office chair. It is useful to be able to adjust the height, and to have larger platforms for bigger pieces. Thin sticks of wood help to raise the piece off the turntable and reduce the likelihood of marking the finish. Longer, thicker battens can be used to extend the table.

DRYING RACKS

Especially in a cramped workshop, drying racks are handy for stacking panels and chairs. Make a homemade rack, using 2 x 2 in. (50 x 50 mm) timber, with long feet to which uprights are joined by angle brackets. Use doweling for the arms, fixing them into holes drilled in the uprights.

CLEANING FACILITIES

Make sure there are cleaning facilities in the workshop. Never pour waste finishes or cleaning material into drains. Keep a sealable metal container for waste materials, and take it to an approved site for disposal. Spray-gun manufacturers provide special brushes for cleaning spraying equipment, but a good supply of rags is useful too. Cellulose thinners will clean all modern finishes, so always have plenty to hand. Rather than continually opening large containers, decant thinners and finish into smaller, more manageable bottles, using a funnel.

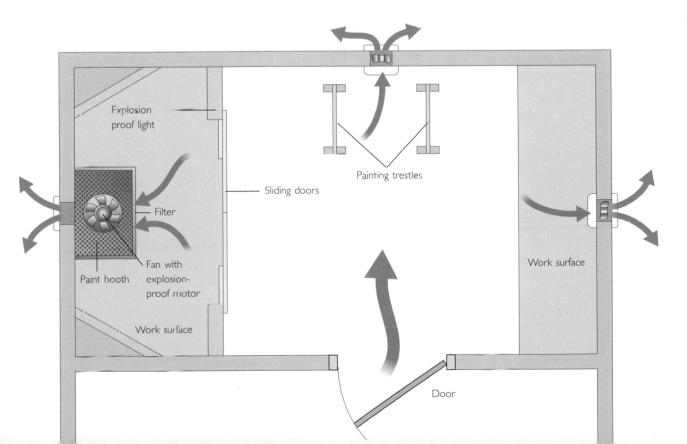

Explosion proof light

Painting trestles

Sliding doors

Filter

Fan with explosion-proof motor

Paint booth

Work surface

Work surface

Door

SEE ALSO
Preparation, pages 24–71
Start spraying, page 142

CHOOSING SPRAY FINISHES

There is a wide choice of finishes available for spraying, but they largely fall into one of these four categories, and it is worth taking a look at their relative benefits and shortcomings before deciding which kind of finish will be most suitable to apply on each workpiece. Always read the instructions supplied with your chosen finish, and follow them accurately in order to get the most out of the product, as ratios and specific cautions will vary from manufacturer to manufacturer.

SPRAY TINTS

Spray tints are ready-mixed with cellulose, though they can be further diluted with the appropriate finish. Sometimes called cellulose colors, they are powerful—so use them in small quantities. They are the most suitable option for shading (see page 149), for which they are best used after the first sealer coat.

NITROCELLULOSE FINISHES

Nitrocellulose is the oldest of modern spray finishes. It was first used at the beginning of this century as "dope" to stretch and strengthen the canvas covering of early airplanes. It was favored for its quick-drying qualities. The cellulose compound, which remains a base ingredient of many spray finishes, is extracted from the cotton plant.

Nitrocellulose finishes are about the simplest to spray because they are used directly from the can, without having to mix them with a catalyst. Only add thinners to nitrocellulose finishes when they are not atomizing properly—and even then they should be thinned by no more than 10 percent. Globules of finish on the surface are evidence of the lacquer being too thick.

USING NITROCELLULOSE FINISHES

Before spraying, seal the timber by hand with a shellac sanding sealer and leave to dry for 30 minutes before lightly sanding with fine silicon-carbide paper. Do not use more than one coat of any sealer.

Spray the first coat and leave to dry for about 20 minutes before sanding it and applying the next coat. It takes two or three hours before nitrocellulose finish is ready for burnishing. For a quick, cheap, finish one coat is sufficient, but a thin-flow coat on top adds depth and strength.

PROS	CONS
• Moderate cost.	• Susceptible to "chilling" (moisture can cause surface whiteness).
• Fast drying.	
• Easy application.	• Sensitive to temperature—needs at least 65°F (18°C).
	• Not resistant to water.
	• Unsuitable for exterior use.

ACID-CATALYST FINISHES

The great advantage of acid-catalyst finishes is that they are hard-wearing, being especially popular for tabletops. The main drawback to acid-catalyst finishes is that they have to be mixed with a catalyst, which adds to the setting-up time, and needs to be handled carefully, wearing protective gloves. The power of acid-catalyst finishes does have detrimental effects upon stains and some timbers. Brown oil stains are often turned red by these finishes, and red streaks are sometimes produced in sycamore and certain fruitwoods, such as pear.

USING ACID-CATALYST FINISHES

Clean the piece well before spraying and seal with a shellac sanding sealer when refinishing old wood. Make sure stain is completely dry before applying the finish.

Resin-bound grain fillers are compatible with acid-catalyst finishes; oil-bound fillers should be avoided. Acid-catalyst finishes have a high solid content, so will fill the grain to a greater extent than other spraying lacquers.

The proportion of catalyst to base varies, but adding more catalyst than recommended does not speed up the curing time and will produce a brittle finish. If you use too little catalyst, then the finish will not cure at all, so always follow the instructions provided with the finish.

When spraying acid-catalyst finishes, try not to apply it as thick as other finishes. Turn down the flow rate slightly, and sweep a little faster with the gun.

An acid-catalyst finish takes 1/2–1 1/2 hours to dry, and can be recoated as soon as it is touch dry, but note that the finish will continue to get harder over seven days, so leave burnishing for as long as possible.

PROS	CONS
• Hard-wearing.	• Slow to cure.
• Resistant to abrasions and to some acids and alkalis.	• Vulnerable to wet heat.
• Dries clear, no yellowing.	

Spraying on finishes gives a good, even glow that can be hard to achieve by hand. This chair is pictured before (right) and after (left) being sprayed with a clear nitrocellulose lacquer.

PAINT FINISHES

Nitrocellulose and acid-catalyst finishes are available in paint form for special effects, such as splatter (see page 148), and also for simple painted surfaces. Contrary to the popular view that paints hide defects, paints actually highlight errors more than any other finish. A black finish is the most difficult to produce and the least forgiving.

USING PAINT FINISHES

Use a nitrocellulose or acid-catalyst pigmented finish for interiors, and polyurethane for outdoors.

Preparation must be faultless. When grain filling, which is often necessary, use an oil-bound filler before spraying with nitrocellulose; otherwise, use either a resin-bound or an oil-bound filler.

Once the surface is perfect, apply an undercoat. Finishing suppliers sell special undercoats, which are cheaper than thinning down the finish coat and are specifically formulated to aid adhesion. Leave the undercoat to dry for about one hour, then flat down with fine silicon-carbide abrasive paper. Make sure the surface is thoroughly dusted down, since the smallest speck or hair will show up later. Apply the finishing coat, in either gloss or matte. If necessary, spray on further coats before burnishing.

PROS	CONS
• Available in a range of colors.	• Dry more slowly than clear lacquers.
• Will mask discoloration in timber.	• Exaggerate woodworking and spraying defects, and are sensitive to dust.
• Can be used for special effects.	• Faultless preparation is required.
	• Before spraying with them, your gun needs to be cleaned very thoroughly.

WATERBORNE FINISHES

With most spray finishes, the solid element is carried from the gun to the surface by a petroleum-based solvent, which then evaporates. It therefore made sense to try to discover a solvent that was inexpensive and environmentally harmless. The answer was water.

Waterborne finishes have a flatter, more natural appearance than other lacquers. As a result, they are a common choice for Scandinavian-style pine products. You can buy waterborne finishes in either one- or two-part form. In the latter type a cross-linker is used as the hardener, and the manufacturer's instructions should be followed carefully when mixing. Store waterborne finishes in a frost-free cupboard.

USING WATERBORNE FINISHES

If staining, use water-based stains. A waterborne sealer should be used prior to spraying. Before applying the sealer, dampen the surface to raise the grain, then let it dry and sand it lightly. Do not use a grain filler when working with waterborne finishes, because adhesion is not always satisfactory.

Waterborne finishes are not compatible with other spray finishes. The gun and other equipment must therefore be absolutely clean before use, otherwise the finish is likely to foam. When spraying, turn the fluid rate down. Most solvents evaporate to some degree between the gun and the surface, but this is not the case with waterborne finishes—so try to use thin coats and keep the viscosity up in order to avoid runs.

PROS	CONS
• Not harmful to the environment.	• Comparatively expensive.
• Do not constitute a fire hazard.	• Difficult to use, since they tend to sag or run.
	• Sensitive to cold, and are easily contaminated by other finishes.
	• Grain filler cannot be used with them.

SEE ALSO
Spray guns, page 134
Choosing spray finishes, page 140

START SPRAYING

There are four adjustments to any type of spray gun. However, the air flow adjuster normally stays fully open all the time, as it is much easier to alter air pressure at the air regulator (see page 138) where there is a gauge. This is useful for adjusting the size of the particles borne in the air flow. Most finishes run at 30 to 35 1b psi (2 bars), but by cutting the pressure right back, splattering effects (see page 148) can be achieved.

YOU WILL NEED

Spray gun
Compressor and air regulator
Goggles, mask or respirator, overalls, and protective gloves
Spray booth
Sealable metal container for waste
Spray finishes and thinners

The spread adjuster is much more important, as it regulates the quantity of air flowing out of the horn holes in the cap and so changes the shape of the stream. With this valve fully open the flow is a very flat ellipse. The flow returns to a funnel shape about 2 in. (50 mm) wide when the air is cut off from the horn holes. Use a wide ellipse (as wide as the gun will allow) for flat surfaces and a more cylindrical flow for rails, legs, and narrow surfaces.

It is also possible to adjust the fluid flow carrying the finish. This is done by limiting the travel of the trigger, which restricts the needle's movement away from the nozzle. Close up the fluid adjuster for finishes that have been thinned for easy flow; open it up for heavy pigmented finishes. If runs appear on the surface, too much material is being applied.

The final adjustment is to direct the fan of finish vertically or horizontally. With the horn holes horizontal, the fan will be vertical. Most of the time you will be spraying from side to side, and so want the finish to be directed in a vertical swathe, as if you were painting with a flat brush. You will therefore only need to alter the setting when you are going to spray up and down.

ADJUSTING A SPRAY GUN

01 Adjust the needle travel to alter the flow of material from the gun.

02 Unscrew the knurled knob to allow more material out of the gun, and tighten to restrict the flow.

03 Test the flow of material through the gun, and keep adjusting the needle stop until the required flow is achieved. Spray a piece of scrap as a test. If the coat is heavy and runs, too much material is being used. If the surface does not look wet, not enough lacquer is passing from the nozzle.

HEALTH AND SAFETY

When spraying, always wear goggles and a mask or, if possible, a respirator.

Wear protective gloves when working with acid-catalyst finishes. Wear overalls at all times.

USEFUL INFORMATION

APPROPRIATE FINISHES
Do not use shellac finishes with a spray gun, as they tend to cobweb.

COMMON PROBLEMS
Spraying too close or with too much fluid causes runs.

Spraying too far away or with too much air results in a thin, uneven finish.

DRYING TIMES
Most spray finishes are dry within 20 minutes, though some take hours or days to cure fully.

USING A SPRAY GUN

Modern finishes are popular not only for their qualities of resistance, but also because they can be applied consistently at an economic rate. Indeed, a professional spray finisher will say that a consistent finish is the most important characteristic of a job done well. Some practice is needed in order to fully grasp the formula for a fine finish and to master the hand-to-eye coordination needed to work with a spray gun. Even so, you will be surprised how easy and quick it is to get started—and you will soon appreciate the potential of a spraying system.

The important variables to experiment with are the fluid, spread, and air supply adjustments on the gun and air regulator, and the viscosity of finish being used. There is no benefit to be gained from high air pressure, because high pressure makes the air and atomized finish bounce back onto the finisher—so keep the pressure as low as possible, without creating globules of finish. About 30 lb psi (2 bars) is sufficient for most finishes. If the flow of fluid is too fast, you will be unable to keep up and the finish will start to run. Always use two or more thin applications, rather than one thick coat.

The distance between the gun and the surface, together with the smoothness of the sweep as you are spraying, is critical for the finish. This is where the skill of the finisher really tells. Generally, unless the manufacturer of the finish recommends otherwise, spray with the gun about 8 in. (200 mm) from the surface. Too near will result in runs; too far spreads the finish too wide.

KEEPING THE SPRAY CONSISTENT

Consistent spraying is accomplished with smooth, steady sweeps of the gun, parallel to the surface. When learning to spray there is an almost irresistible tendency to keep the wrist firm, as if putting in golf. When putting, the arms form an arc, with the hands further from the ground at the beginning and end of each stroke than at the moment when the club hits the ball. So, if you keep your wrist rigid when spraying, the part of the work closest to you will receive a thick coat of finish (often with runs), whereas the areas furthest away from you will be more thinly coated.

The trick is to flex your wrist as your arm moves. Try not to move your body unless absolutely necessary, since this will upset the consistency of the sweep—only move your arms. The aim is to keep the spray gun parallel with the surface all the time. Flex your wrist as if ironing a pair of trousers or painting a door.

SPRAYING METHODS

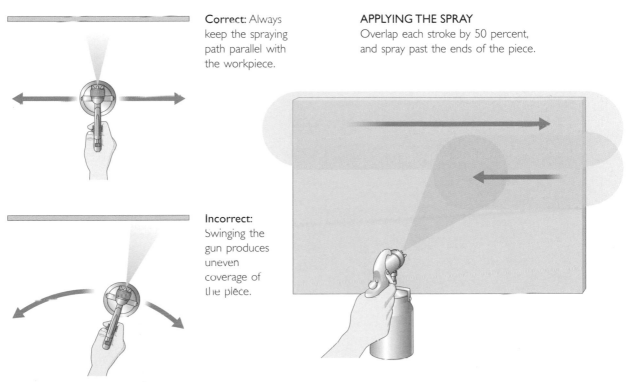

Correct: Always keep the spraying path parallel with the workpiece.

Incorrect: Swinging the gun produces uneven coverage of the piece.

APPLYING THE SPRAY
Overlap each stroke by 50 percent, and spray past the ends of the piece.

SPRAYING A CHAIR

Before starting to spray, check the spread adjustment on the gun. Test this by spraying on a piece of scrap wood or against the side of the booth. A wide fan, which is ideal for spraying a tabletop, would produce too much overspray on the rails and legs of a chair, so reduce the amount of air channeled to the horn holes; and spray in a cone-shaped fan, spreading to about 2 in. (50 mm) as it hits the surface.

It does not matter how you spray rounded chair legs and rails, but try not to point the spray gun directly at the face of square components. Instead, position the gun so that it is aiming at an edge and two faces. This way you can spray both faces simultaneously, which saves time and consumes less finish. However, do not use this method when spraying components wider than about 1 1/2 in. (40 mm), as that may result in an uneven finish.

HOW MANY COATS?

Depending on the effect or protection required, one or two coats of finish will be sufficient. It varies from one piece to another. An average-size kitchen tabletop will need about 1 1/3 pt (700 cc) for spraying both sides with one coat of finish, while a chair will need about 1 pt (500 cc).

Spray finishes dry quickly (within 20 minutes), but take longer to cure. It is important to apply the second coat as soon as possible after the first—once the surface is touch dry and has been lightly sanded—so that it can bite in before the curing process starts.

ORDER OF WORK

When spraying a chair, start with the legs. Spray the inside of a leg first **(1)**, then the outside **(2)**. Spray the rails **(3)** in the same manner. Next, spray the outside (i.e. back) of the chair's backrest **(4)**, then the front of the backrest **(5)**, and last of all the seat **(6)**.

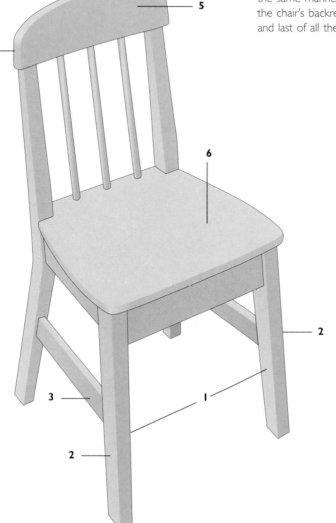

HINTS AND TIPS

- Test colors by spraying them on scrap wood (if possible, similar to the timber of the workpiece), to get a true idea of the finish.
- Always spray parallel to the surface, flexing the wrist and keeping the gun an even distance from the workpiece. Most finishes should be sprayed about 8 in. (200 mm) from the surface.
- Always use two or more thin applications, rather than one thick coat.
- Keep the air pressure as low as possible, and the fluid flow at a rate you can keep up with.
- On wide surfaces, overlap each sweep of the gun by about 50 percent.
- Continue each sweep beyond the end of the piece to ensure complete coverage.

AIMING A SPRAY GUN

When spraying a curved chair leg, spray directly at the center of the piece, using a narrow fan shape. For square-shaped legs, direct the spray at the corners of the piece, again with a narrow fan shape.

SPRAYING A TABLE

When you are spraying, there is always going to be some overspray that does not hit the desired spot. Most will be sucked out by the extraction system, but some of this material is bound to fall upon areas already finished. Do not, however, be frightened to overspray at the end of each sweep, and do not be tempted to take the pressure off the trigger. A constant flow of finish is vital, even if,

momentarily, the gun is not aimed at the surface. It is important to start and end each sweep with the spray at full blast. Do not alter the flow with the trigger. Instead, adjust the gun. Always spray with the trigger full on. To ensure an even coat across a wide surface, such as a tabletop, overlap each sweep by about 50 percent.

ORDER OF WORK

Because some overspray will fall on finished components, leave the most visible parts until last and start with the most inconspicuous areas. On a table, that means spraying the inside of the legs (**1**) or underframe (**2**) first, and then the outside (**3**). When it comes to the tabletop, always spray the edges first (**4**), even though they are more obvious to the eye than the underneath. This is because more overspray is created when spraying the edges than when working on the bottom or top. After the edges, spray the bottom (**5**) and, finally, the top (**6**).

Finishing with spray is rather like veneering. If only one side is sprayed, it may "cup" (distort) due to the pull of the drying finish, so always finish both sides, even if the top is fixed in place.

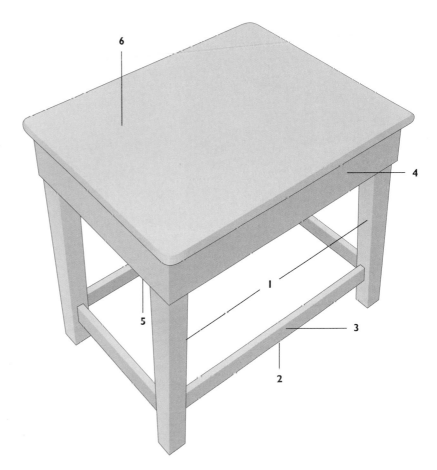

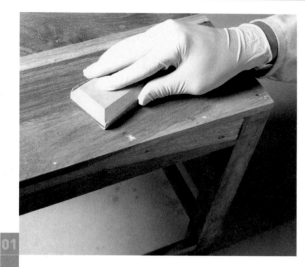

01 Prepare the surface of the piece to be sprayed by sanding all over with a medium-grade abrasive paper.

02 Seal all surfaces using a precatalyzed sanding sealer and allow to dry.

03 Denib the surfaces using a flexible silicon carbide pad until smooth. Wipe off the dust with a tack rag.

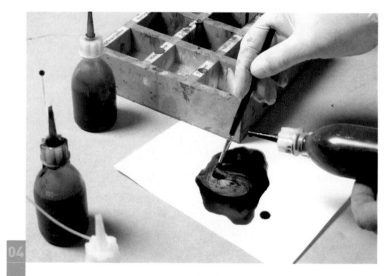

04 Using an artists' brush on a sheet of white paper, mix pigments and spirit dyes to match the color of the wood surface.

05 Use the artists' brush and pigment and spirit dye mix to obliterate any small, filled areas, so that they blend in with the rest of the piece.

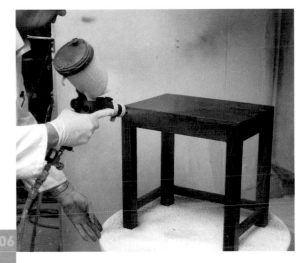

06 Use a small spray gun to apply overall color.

07 Control the trigger on the spray gun to get in close and blend in lighter areas. Allow to dry.

08 Apply a finishing coat of gloss precatalyzed lacquer and allow to dry.

09

The table has a very professional finish, and was completed quickly.

SEE ALSO
Spray guns, page 134
Choosing spray finishes, page 140

CREATING SPECIAL SPRAY EFFECTS

Special effects with spray guns fall into two categories: those that require creative use of the gun and its adjustments, and those that are determined by special materials. In both cases, it is possible to achieve similar effects by hand—but, with practice, you will find spraying quicker.

YOU WILL NEED

Spray finishes and thinners (see page 140)
Spray gun
Compressor and air regulator
Goggles, mask or respirator, overalls, and protective gloves
Spray booth
Undercoat
Base coat
Silicon-carbide abrasive paper
Sealable metal container for waste

SPLATTER FINISHES

Splatter finishes are among the easiest of creative spray effects to produce. By hand, surfaces can be splattered with a toothbrush, creating an irregular speckled pattern. The same results can be achieved in the spraying shop, by adjusting the air pressure, fluttering the trigger, and altering the distance between gun and surface.

When using a spray gun, globules of finish are dropped onto the surface by turning down the air pressure at the air regulator. This means that, instead of the finish being atomized into a thin spray, the material falls on the workpiece in droplets.

Any type of paint or pigmented finishes, which are available from finishing suppliers, can be used for the base coat and the splattering. Pastel colors are normally best for the background, with brighter splattering on top. There are no strict rules to follow, and you may find that other color combinations suit the situation better.

01 Make sure the surface is thoroughly prepared, in accordance with the paint finish you will be using. Apply one layer of undercoat and then the required base, sanding with silicon-carbide abrasive paper between coats.

02 Fill the spray-gun canister with the splatter finish mixed to the same viscosity as the base coat. The finish must not be mixed too thinly, otherwise it will continue to atomize without forming the characteristic splatter globules.

03 Turn down the air pressure at the air regulator until it is just sufficient to atomize the finish. Test this on a piece of scrap wood. By pulling the trigger further back, more material will flow to the nozzle, creating a thicker splatter pattern.

01 Prepare the surface according to the spray finish you are using and stain the piece using a water-based or alcohol stain. Stain to the color required for the lightest areas. Seal this with a shellac sealer, then sand gently with 320 grit silicon-carbide paper and dust off.

02 Use spray tints for the shading. Mix to a color about half a shade darker than the original stain. The trick is to use a tint that is not too dark, otherwise it becomes very difficult to produce gradual shading from light to dark. The aim is to avoid any sharp definition between shaded and unshaded areas.

03 Darken those areas that are most likely to collect dust with age, building up the color in recesses and internal corners with coats of spray tint. Finish with a matte nitrocellulose lacquer.

HEALTH AND SAFETY

- When spraying, always wear goggles and a mask or, if possible, a respirator.
- Wear protective gloves when working with acid-catalyst finishes.
- Wear overalls at all times.

SHADING

While either suction- or gravity feed guns can be used for a splattered finish, the latter are best for shading because they are much easier to manipulate when trying to replicate the aged look produced by rubbing (see pages 14–15). Though it may take time to develop the skills necessary for accurate shading (especially for creating darker areas in corners and recesses), you will find that shading of a panel from the center outward is as easy as by hand.

HAMMER FINISH

The reason a hammer finish is so named is not because a blunt instrument is used to distress the surface, but because the finish resembles hammered pewter or metal. It is a special effect used to make surfaces look metallic. The effect hides the grain of the piece, so while it can be used perfectly well on elaborately grained timber, it is a pity to hide the character of an attractive wood and medium-density fiberboard is probably the best surface on which to work.

A hammered finish is produced by two spraying applications. The first coat is a cellulose spray based on an aluminum paste, to give the metallic content. This is followed by a splattered coat of ethyl acetate (the appropriate solvent) at low pressure, to break up the aluminum and create the hammered look.

Some skill is required to produce a hammered finish, because the distance of the spray gun from the surface is another factor that determines the degree of hammer. With the gun close to the workpiece, the splatter will be wider.

Hammer finish is sold in a variety of colors, and can be mixed with spray tints. Blues, reds, yellows, and greens are all popular colors for a hammer effect. Although it is possible to mix your own hammer finish in the workshop, it is more realistic to purchase it ready-made. However, it is expensive and for that reason it is mainly used for small items.

01 Remember when preparing the surface that you are trying to achieve a metallic effect, so the surface needs to be exceptionally smooth. Apply the first cellulose spray coat. Leave for 5 to 10 minutes until tacky.

02 Apply a splattered coat of ethyl acetate (the appropriate solvent) at low pressure. The lower the pressure—e.g. 5–10 1b psi (0.5 bar)—the wider the pattern will be. Higher pressure—10–15 1b psi (1 bar)—produces a tighter effect.

03 Try to keep the distance constant, so you produce a consistent hammer effect. If necessary, protect with nitrocellulose or acid-catalyst spray once the finish is dry, which takes about two hours.

SUNBURST EFFECTS

You may be excused for mistaking sunburst for shading. The effect is similar, though sunburst is used for decoration as opposed to reproduction and restoration. It is popular on guitars, car dashboards, and wooden surfaces that have to blend in with plastic and metal. It is a flamboyant finish, and some artistic flair is needed in order to achieve an attractive result. Stunning effects can be produced with bright yellows, greens, and reds; or more subtle effects with browns and wood colors.

01

Guitars and dashboards are the most common objects for a sunburst finish. Make sure the surface is flat and smooth before starting the spraying operation, removing any blemishes where necessary.

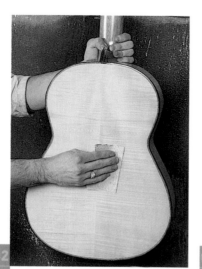

02
Use fine self-lubricating silicon-carbide abrasive paper for the final sanding. Always sand with the grain, holding the paper flat in the hand.

03
Apply the base stain, using a spraying or alcohol stain. Choose a color that is lighter than the finished color required. Keep the coat as even as possible. If you have a choice of spray guns, use a gravity-feed type for this operation.

04
Start applying the darker shading spray, gradually building up the color from the outer edges of the guitar. The principle of producing the brightest areas in the center of panels is true for the majority of pieces.

05 Build up the shading, blending it with the lighter areas. Although the aim is to produce a darker ring around the edges, it is important that there is no obvious line between dark and light. Build up the shading slowly, rather than applying a single, heavy coat.

06 Protect the sunburst effect with two even coats of clear lacquer. Denib between applications. Dashboards are often sprayed with a high-gloss finish, but it is equally appropriate to use semi-gloss or matte lacquers.

07 The finished guitar, showing the gradual shading from light to dark. In this case, the sunburst finish has been used as decoration, but it can also be used to imitate the rubbed quality of older pieces.

TROUBLESHOOTING

It is often said that one of the skills of the finisher is the knack of remedying a fault without it showing. The ideal is, of course, not to make any mistakes—and prevention is always better than cure!

The more traditional finishes are often reversible, which means they can be removed fairly easily, without recourse to stripping or sanding back. Spray finishes are tougher, and are usually nonreversible. As a result, stripping may be the only cure for a major mistake.

HINTS AND TIPS

- Always leave the finish to dry before attempting to deal with faults.
- Apply thin coats of finish, rather than fewer thick coats.
- Always use materials as specified by the suppliers.
- Before taking remedial action, think out what may have gone wrong and check possible causes.

TRADITIONAL FINISHING FAULTS

Although some faults in traditional finishes are due to workshop conditions or the material itself, the majority are caused by human error. Practice is therefore the most effective preventive measure. Fortunately, most traditional finishes (with the exception of varnishes) are reversible and can be rubbed off, without having to resort to stripping and starting again. Oiling and waxing are relatively straightforward finishes, compared with French polishing. The lack of faults cataloged here for those methods reflects their ease of application.

BLOOMING

SYMPTOM: A film of condensation appears in the finished surface.
CAUSE: Humidity in the workshop.
CURE: Sand back and rework.
PREVENTION: Check the level of humidity in your workshop and make sure there is adequate ventilation. If necessary, buy a dehumidifier.

BLUSHING

SYMPTOM: A dull whiteness, which can appear in any type of finish.
CAUSE: Damp, cold workshop conditions.
CURE: Cut back and rework.
PREVENTION: Check workshop for damp, and make sure the temperature is not below 65°F (18°C).

CHILLING

SYMPTOM: Appears as a dull, white semi-opaque film.
CAUSE: Cold workshop conditions.
CURE: Repolish the surface using a little denatured alcohol in the polishing pad.
PREVENTION: Ensure the temperature in the workshop does not drop below 65°F (18°C).

CRACKING

SYMPTOM: Thin cracks show up in the surface after some time has elapsed.
CAUSE: Linseed oil buried under the finish.
CURE: Gently sand the surface with fine abrasive and repolish. If there is extensive cracking, cut back with denatured alcohol and rework.
PREVENTION: Use less linseed oil on the polishing pad and avoid burying oil under heavy coats of polish.

CRAZING

SYMPTOM: Very fine cracks on the surface.
CAUSE: Too much oil has been used to lubricate the polishing pad.
CURE: Sand back with fine abrasive paper and repolish. If the crazing is severe, strip off the polish and repolish.
PREVENTION: Before tackling the surface with the pad, ensure excess oil is worked out by pressing the pad down on a scrap of paper or spare piece of timber.

FATTY EDGES

SYMPTOM: Polish builds up along the edges of tabletops and the corners of legs.
CAUSE: As the polishing pad is squeezed over the edges, polish builds up there.
CURE: Rub down with fine abrasive paper, then touch up and repolish.
PREVENTION: Use the polishing pad to remove excess polish before it builds up.

FLAKING

SYMPTOM: Finish breaks up.
CAUSE: Too much oil in filler or stain.
CURE: Strip back, then brush out filler and start again.
PREVENTION: Make sure the filler or stain is compatible with the finish.

ROPY SURFACE

SYMPTOM: Waves are visible on the surface after polishing, often in tight circles like ripples. Can also look like rope.
CAUSE: Misuse of polishing pad.
CURE: Cut back with denatured alcohol in the polishing pad.
PREVENTION: Make sure an even pressure is maintained when using the pad. Work with circular motions, trying to keep the pressure the same as you move the polishing pad away from and toward the body.

SWEATING

SYMPTOM: Polish remains sticky, even after some time has elapsed.
CAUSE: Linseed oil has been trapped under the finish, or old white, transparent, or French polish has been used.
CURE: Cut back the finish with denatured alcohol in the polishing pad, then leave the surface to dry and rework the finish.
PREVENTION: Use less linseed oil to lubricate the polishing pad, and avoid burying oil under heavy coats of polish.

WHITE EDGES

SYMPTOM: Edges look as if they are white, where the stain has been worn away.
CAUSE: The surface has been sanded clumsily after applying a water-based stain.
CURE: Apply polish as normal, then touch up with alcohol colors or pigments once the surface is completely dry.
PREVENTION: Take care when sanding stained surfaces, avoiding pressing too hard.

WHITE IN THE GRAIN

SYMPTOM: White flecks in the grain, under the finish.
CAUSE: Grain filler has not dried, or is too light.
CURE: Rub off polish with denatured alcohol; clean off oil and wax with mineral spirits. Then work out the filler with a stiff brush.
PREVENTION: Make sure filler is dry, or use darker filler.

WHIPS

SYMPTOM: Polish builds up in ridges, often in circles following the path of the polishing pad.
CAUSE: The polishing pad is too wet.
CURE: Leave to dry. Then sand with fine abrasive, or use a pad with a little denatured alcohol and work until the surface has been leveled.
PREVENTION: Avoid charging the pad with too much polish.

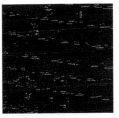
Blooming

Chilling

Cracking

Crazing

Sweating

White in grain

SPRAY FINISHING FAULTS

Spray finishes are tougher than the traditional finishes, so remedying mistakes usually requires stripping. You therefore need to be aware of the preventive measures that can be taken to reduce the likelihood of faults.

AERATION

SYMPTOM: Small bubbles appear, creating a milky effect.

POSSIBLE CAUSES: Too heavy a coat of lacquer (which traps air or solvent under the surface); or too much air pressure, which can dry the surface too quickly for solvent to evaporate or air to escape.

CURE: Spray on a wet-flow coat; or pull over the surface and then respray.

PREVENTION: Keep spray gun moving, and make sure it is not too close to the surface.

AIR LEAKS

SYMPTOM: Air hisses out of air holes in air cap.

POSSIBLE CAUSES: Foreign matter in valve; worn or damaged air valve; broken air-valve spring; valve stem needs lubrication; bent valve stem; packing nut too tight; casket damaged or omitted.

CURE: Check and repair parts.

PREVENTION: Maintain and clean spray gun regularly.

BLISTERING

SYMPTOM: Small blisters on the surface.

CAUSE: Water or grease in the air line getting into the atomized material.

CURE: Sand surface and respray.

PREVENTION: Clean air line and drain transformer.

BLOOMING

SYMPTOM: Film of condensation on the surface.

CAUSE: Humidity in the workshop.

CURE: Strip surface and start again.

PREVENTION: Use a dehumidifier in the workshop, and keep the area well ventilated.

BLUSHING

SYMPTOM: A dull whiteness appears in the coat.

CAUSE: Damp workshop conditions.

CURE: Strip surface and start again.

PREVENTION: Keep minimum temperature above 65°F (18°C); insulate workshop to reduce humidity.

CISSING

SYMPTOM: Small circular patches, resembling miniature volcanoes.

CAUSE: Grease or silicone in the finish repels subsequent coats.

CURE: Deep sand and respray.

PREVENTION: Prepare surface thoroughly before beginning to spray.

FLAKING

SYMPTOM: Film of finish breaks down with time.

CAUSE: Too much oil in a stain or filler.

CURE: Strip and respray.

PREVENTION: Check that lacquer is compatible with filler or stain.

FLUID LEAKS

SYMPTOM: The finish leaks out through the nozzle of the gun.

POSSIBLE CAUSES: Dirty or worn fluid tip and nozzle; obstruction causing improper seating of needle; needle packing-nut too tight; broken fluid-needle spring; wrong needle.

CURE: Check, and adjust or replace part.

PREVENTION: Clean spray gun thoroughly, and lubricate moving parts.

FLUTTERING SPRAY

SYMPTOM: Air and material flow is hesitant or jerky.

POSSIBLE CAUSES: Insufficient material in container; canister tipped too far; fluid passage blocked; cracked fluid tube in canister; damaged tip or nozzle; material too heavy; clogged air vent in cup lid; damaged hose or dirty coupling nut; fault in trigger adjustment.

CURE: Check and mend part, or thin the material.

PREVENTION: Keep spray gun well maintained, and clean it thoroughly after use. Mix lacquer according to the manufacturer's instructions.

ORANGE-PEEL EFFECT

SYMPTOM: A slight ripple effect is left on the surface, like orange or lemon peel.

POSSIBLE CAUSES: Spraying too close to the surface; application too thick.

CURE: Rub the surface flat with progressive grades of abrasive, then recoat.

PREVENTION: Keep correct distance between gun and surface, about 8 in. (200 mm), all the time; thin the lacquer, but without using too much thinner.

OVERSPRAY

SYMPTOM: The surface feels rough because the spray lies on the surface, forming small particles of dry paint or lacquer.

CAUSE: Insufficient care when using the spray gun.

CURE: Lightly sand the surface with fine abrasive paper, and respray.

PREVENTION: Trigger off after each stroke or pass. Use low air pressure.

PINHOLES

SYMPTOM: Tiny indentations or pinpricks are formed in the surface of the lacquer as it dries.

CAUSE: The lacquer is applied too heavily, which means that solvents are trapped underneath the surface and have to rise to the top to evaporate.

CURE: Sand back the surface and start again.

PREVENTION: Mix a thinner coat of lacquer; move the spray gun faster across the surface and increase the distance between gun and workpiece.

RUNS

SYMPTOM: The finish runs down the surface.

POSSIBLE CAUSES: Holding the gun too close: applying too much material in one place; spraying over the same area twice.

CURE: Leave to dry, then sand down with fine silicon-carbide paper before respraying.

PREVENTION: Hold gun further from surface; practice a consistent sweep over the piece, overlapping by no more than 50 percent on each sweep.

SPRAYFOG

SYMPTOM: Spray comes out of the gun as a mist.

POSSIBLE CAUSES: Material too thin; air pressure too high; gun held too far from surface.

PREVENTION: Add more base coat—or start again, using less thinner; reduce air pressure at regulator; hold gun closer to surface.

WHITE IN THE GRAIN

SYMPTOM: White flecks under the finish.

CAUSE: Filler has not dried thoroughly, or the fault has been caused by incompatibility between the filler and the finish.

CURE: Strip and respray.

PREVENTION: Make sure excess filler is cleaned off, and that it is completely dry before spraying.

WRINKLING OR CRACKING

SYMPTOM: Unwanted cracks or wrinkles appear in the finish.

CAUSE: When a second coat of lacquer is applied before the first has dried properly, the two finishes dry at different rates.

CURE: Sand and respray; or strip and start again if the cracks are deep.

PREVENTION: Check the finish manufacturer's instructions for drying, thinning, and curing. Make sure the first coat is dry before applying the second.

Blistering

Cissing

Orange-peel effect

Overspray

Pinholes

White in grain

GLOSSARY

Acetic acid (white vinegar)
Used to neutralize two-part bleaches.

Acid-catalyst lacquer A lacquer usually based on urea-formaldehyde and melamine that cures chemically after the addition of a hardener. Can be applied with a brush, spray, or roller. Available in clear, gloss, and matte, and may be colored.

Bars Metric measure of pressure.

Beveling Taking off sharp edges with a plane or chisel.

Binder This is the solid content of a varnish or lacquer remaining after the solvent has evaporated and which forms the film, and if pigments are added binds them to the surface.

Chemical stripping The procedure of removing old finishes using solvent, paint, and varnish removers, or strong alkaline solutions. Hot-air guns may also be used but may scorch the wood.

Clamping Using a clamp for pressure when gluing joints and repairing blisters.

Cleat A small nail or screw used to hold down a panel on the bench while the panel is being worked on.

Cobweb A spraying fault that occurs when sprayed shellac materials do not atomize properly and form a cobweb pattern on the surface.

Cold cure See Acid-catalyst lacquer.

Creep The way stain is absorbed along the grain.

Cross grain Grain structure that runs at an angle to the main grain direction. Sanding across the grain is usually to be avoided.

Cut back Rubbing a finish with fine abrasive paper until the finish is flat and smooth.

Danish oil An oil finish that cures by oxidation (reaction with oxygen). Particularly useful for oily timbers.

Denibbing Rubbing with a fine abrasive paper to remove any small particles of foreign matter that stand proud on a dry surface coating.

Distressing Making a piece of furniture look old by bruising the surface and giving it a faded appearance.

Doping Application of dope, which is a mixture of stain, pigment, and French polish, using a mop or brush to make a semi-transparent color.

Dye A translucent color that is dissolved in a medium and used as a stain.

Fad A pear-shaped piece of batting used to apply French polish to nooks and crannies, and also as the core of a polishing pad.

Fadding Applying French polish with a fad before bodying up.

Fillers Materials used to fill holes and deep bruises. Available as wax, shellac, and two-part varieties.

Flogging brush Used for woodgraining effects, it has long bristles that, when struck against the glaze, produce a pattern similar to that seen in the grain of the wood.

French polish Shellac and denatured alcohol mixed to produce a polish, also supplied as garnet, white, button, and transparent polish.

French polishing General term referring to the application of shellac polish with a polishing pad.

Glaze A transparent or translucent coating material, sometimes colored, applied over a base color and used for special effects like graining and marbling.

Grain fillers A mixture of filling powder, binder, solvent, and pigments applied with burlap to fill the pores in timber.

Green copperas A chemical stain used to produce green to gray hues.

Grit grades Sizes of grit used on abrasive papers. High numbers, such as 360, refer to fine grit while 80 is a coarse abrasive.

Heartwood The center of a log that has stopped growing, and is usually darker and harder than the outer layer of sapwood.

Keying Abrading the surface of a finish to roughen it as a base for further coats of finish.

Medium density fiberboard (MDF) Fiberboard, similar to chipboard, but denser. Made from wood dust bonded by a resin.

Medullary rays Grain pattern in oak that runs across the grain, contrasting with the rest of the timber. The pattern is enhanced by quarter-sawing the timber.

Mineral spirits Hydrocarbon solvent used to thin oil stains, gold size, and glazes.

Mop Round brush made from soft bristles, supplied in sizes 6–10, used for applying color.

Neutralize To make chemically neutral (neither acidic nor alkaline).

Oiling process of applying oil to produce an oiled finish; for example, Danish or linseed oil applied to teak.

Oxalic acid crystals White crystals used as a mild bleach, when in saturated solution, to clean off iron or blue stains.

Pigments Colors that do not dissolve, but are suspended in a medium to produce opaque colors. Mixed with paints and glazes.

Pigment stain Semi-transparent stain made from finely ground colors that remain in suspension.

Polishing pad A fad wrapped in a white cotton cloth, used for French polishing.

Polyester resin Two-part resin finish, which cures by chemical reaction, with one part acting as a catalyst.

Polymerization This is the chemical reaction that occurs whereby the molecules link, often by cross-linking with various components, to form a polymer. See Acid-catalyst lacquer.

Polyurethane oil Synthetic oil finish.

Proprietary reviver Used for rejuvenating old finishes; sold as polish or finish reviver.

Pumice powder Fine abrasive powder for dulling. Used with a dulling brush.

Raising the grain Wetting timber to expand the cells of the wood before applying a finish.

Sanding sealer A sealer that incorporates a sanding agent to make sanding easier.

Sapwood Layer of timber surrounding the heartwood, which carries the sap through the tree.

Saturated solution When no more solid material can be dissolved in a solution.

Sealing coat First coat of finish used to seal the surface of the timber before applying further coats.

Shellac A resin secreted by the lac beetle, which is only soluble in alcohol or an alkaline solution of water. When dissolved in alcohol it is known as French polish.

Shellac sanding sealer Sealer with shellac base, which includes a sanding agent to fill the pores of the grain.

Silicon-carbide abrasive paper Abrasive paper made from silicon-carbide that uses water as a lubricant. Self-lubricating abrasives incorporate a powder to take away the dust that can scratch the surface.

Skein batting Fine batting covered in thin paper and used as the core of the polishing pad.

Spiriting off Stage of French polishing when the polishing pad is charged with denatured alcohol to produce a gloss finish.

Stain A liquid that will alter the color of wood without leaving a surface film or obscuring the grain. Alcohol stains are made by dissolving analine dyes in denatured alcohol. Oil stains are made from oil-soluble dye stuffs, usually mineral spirits or naphtha. Water-based stains are made from dye stuffs soluble in water.

Stiffing off Stage of French polishing when straight strokes are used, following the grain, with the polishing pad charged with diluted polish and denatured alcohol.

Thinner Solvent used to thin finishes.

Thixotropic agent Additive to paints and varnishes to increase viscosity and prevent pigments settling, and to reduce the chance of runs.

Transparent polish Made from shellac that has been bleached and dewaxed to produce a very pale amber shellac solution.

Tung oil Vegetable oil for oil finishes, also used in some paints and lacquers.

Urea-formaldehyde glue Resin glue used in modern furniture and often supplied in powder form, which is then mixed with water.

Varnish stains Varnish mixed with a dye or pigments and supplied in a range of colors.

Varnish A transparent coating based on a mixture of resins and drying oils and a solvent.

Water-based stain Stain made from water-soluble dyes.

Wax stains Wax and stain combination available in a range of colors, producing a colored wax effect.

Wax sticks Colored wax filler made from wax and pigments, for filling small dents and bruises.

White polish French polish using bleached shellac for natural or light-colored finishes.

INDEX

USEFUL ADDRESSES

Useful names and addresses
The following suppliers offer a mail-order service

Woodworker's Supply
5604 Alameda Pl. N.E., Alberquerque, NM 87113
Telephone: 800 645–9292
http://woodworker.com

Janovic Plaza
30–35 Thomson Avenue
Long Island City   NY 11101
Telephone: 718–392–3999
Fax: 718–784–4564
www.janovic.com

Garrett Wade
161 Avenue of the Americas, New York NY 10013
Telephone (USA and Canada): 800 221 2942
Telephone (International): 212 807 1155
Fax (USA and Canada): 800 566 9525
Fax (International): 212 255 8552
www.garrettwade.com

Wood Finish Supply
P.O. Box 929, Fort Bragg, CA 95437
Telephone (orders): 800–245–5611
Telephone (assistance): 707–962–9480
Fax: 707–962–9484
www.woodfinishsupply.com

CREDITS

Quarto would like to thank and acknowledge the following
for supplying photographs reproduced in this book:

Key: t = top, b = bottom, l = left, r = right

Barlow Tyrie Ltd www.teak.com 21b, 66
Julius Blüthner Pianofortefabrik, photographed by
Jens Dresner 29br
ITW Industrial Finishing, Bournemouth, UK
www.itweuropeanfinishing.com 135, 137, 138

All other photographs and illustrations are the copyright of
Quarto Publishing plc. While every effort has been made to
credit contributors, Quarto would like to apologize should
there have been any omissions or errors – and would be
pleased to make the appropriate correction for future
editions of the book.

PUBLISHER'S NOTE

Working with wood finishes demands care, as some of
the chemicals you will be using are poisonous and/or
corrosive. This means you must take precautions when
you use them; always follow the manufacturer's
instructions; always store chemicals securely in clearly
marked non-food containers and keep them well out of
reach of children. Always wear appropriate protective
attire as recommended by the manufacturer, and ensure
adequate ventilation.

As far as the composition of the finishes mentioned in
this book, the techniques used to apply them , and the
effects they produce are concerned, all statements,
information, and advice given here are believed to be
true and accurate. However, neither the author, copyright
holder, or the publisher can accept any liability for errors
or omisisions.